CHILD-DIRECTED SPEECH IN QAQET

A LANGUAGE OF EAST NEW BRITAIN, PAPUA NEW GUINEA

CHILD-DIRECTED SPEECH IN QAQET
A LANGUAGE OF EAST NEW BRITAIN, PAPUA NEW GUINEA

HENRIKE FRYE

ANU PRESS

ASIA-PACIFIC LINGUISTICS

ANU PRESS

Published by ANU Press
The Australian National University
Canberra ACT 2600, Australia
Email: anupress@anu.edu.au

Available to download for free at press.anu.edu.au

ISBN (print): 9781760465162
ISBN (online): 9781760465179

WorldCat (print): 1332766208
WorldCat (online): 1332763635

DOI: 10.22459/CDSQ.2022

This title is published under a Creative Commons Attribution-NonCommercial-NoDerivatives 4.0 International (CC BY-NC-ND 4.0) licence.

The full licence terms are available at
creativecommons.org/licenses/by-nc-nd/4.0/legalcode

Cover design and layout by ANU Press. Cover photograph *Child in Kamanakam* by Carmen Dawuda.

This book is published under the aegis of the Asia-Pacific Linguistics Editorial Board of ANU Press.

This edition © 2022 ANU Press

Contents

Acknowledgements vii

Part I: Setting the scene

1. Introduction 3
  1.1 Overview 3
  1.2 Child-directed speech 5
  1.3 Qaqet Baining 10
  1.4 Database and methods 16
  1.5 Outlook 20

2. The language environment 21
  2.1 Child rearing practices and frameworks of interaction 21
  2.2 Assessing attitudes 24
  2.3 The amount of input 54
  2.4 Summary: Factors contributing to the language environment
      of children in Raunsepna 60

Part II: Comparison of adult- and child-directed speech

3. Direct comparison of ADS and CDS: The Qaqet pear story corpus 65
  3.1 Methods of data collection 65
  3.2 The data 71

4. Mean length of utterance 83
  4.1 Previous research on MLU in CDS 83
  4.2 Utterances 85
  4.3 Words or morphemes? 87
  4.4 Procedure and results 87
  4.5 Summary: MLU in Qaqet CDS 90

5. Disfluencies 93
  5.1 Previous research on disfluencies in CDS 93
  5.2 A model of disfluency pauses with reference to Qaqet 95
  5.3 Disfluency pauses: Comparison of CDS and ADS 98
  5.4 Distribution of hesitations 101
  5.5 Summary: Disfluencies in Qaqet CDS 104

6.	**Prosodic features**		**107**
	6.1	Previous research on prosodic features of CDS	107
	6.2	Method and results	109
	6.3	Summary: Prosodic features of CDS in Qaqet	120
7.	**Directing attention: Speech acts in Qaqet CDS-narratives**		**123**
	7.1	Previous research on speech acts in CDS	123
	7.2	Data coding and selection	125
	7.3	Functions of regulatory intonation units	128
	7.4	Summary: Fulfilling a common task	137
8.	**Corrective input**		**139**
	8.1	Previous research on corrective input	139
	8.2	Adults' reactions to non-target-like child utterances	140
	8.3	Summary: Imitation and recast	146
9.	**CDS and the Qaqet lexicon**		**149**
	9.1	Previous research on special babytalk words	149
	9.2	Babytalk words in the CDS-pear stories	150
	9.3	Summary	153
10.	**Conclusion**		**155**
	10.1	Hypothesis	155
	10.2	Socio-economic background	156
	10.3	Language attitudes	156
	10.4	The amount of input	157
	10.5	Structural features of Qaqet CDS	158
	10.6	Limitations and future research	160
Appendix: Interview guideline and results			163
References			169
Index			185

Acknowledgements

This work was not produced in empty space, but it was made possible by the immense support I received from many different persons. I want to thank all those people who cared for me and my research and shared their time, ideas and resources with me. You taught me that neither distance nor time pose limits to community and open-mindedness.

First, I am deeply grateful to the communities of Raunsepna, Lamarain and Kamanakam. Thanks for sharing your time, thoughts, stories, your houses, food and buai.

Numerous individuals contributed to this work, be it as participants in audio and video recordings, culture experts, as transcribers or as translators. For their efforts, their lessons, their care, their broad-mindedness and their dedication, I would like to thank:

Afra Kularek, Afra Savangit, Alois Balar, Alois Kemsarlem, Andrew Kaltumen, Angelika Kurlik, Anna Iarilmi, Anna Kaqetki, Anna Mitnik, Anna Savandi, Batlius Kabainga, Ben Karliun, Bernard Kulap, Betty Dangas, Bibiana Mali, Blasius Benga, Blasius Gesaqa, Boniface Lan, Bonifaz Issa, Caroline Unsim, Caspar Mestaqaet, Caspar Panavu, Cecilia Irlus, Christine Maqi, Christopher Kereku, Christopher Mitparlingi, Christopher Philemon, Clement Muaqanem, Clementia Guailas, Damien Kereku, Dorothy Naremitki, Erica Murumgi, Felix Danly, Francis Kalang, Frances Ngeligi, Francisca Ngenara, Francisca Ngusurlki, Gloria Kuanas, Henry Lingisaqa, Jacob Telile, Joana Samisin, Joana Standi, John Landi, Josephine Rami, Lona Sinirang, Lucy Nguingi, Lucy Rluses, Lucy Sutit, Lucy Tena, Lucy Topona, Marcella Tangil, Margret Mitil, Maria Kademgi, Maria Karakmet, Maria Salap, Maria Savarin, Martha Iaken, Martina Lurlki, Mathias Batnaqa, Michael Mestanat, Michael Vaka, Michael Wasupka, Monica Ilas (from Lasrlem), Monica Ilas (from Lualait), Monica Sandi, Monica Sunun, Patrick Lemigel, Paul Alin,

Paula Nuvaqat, Peter Saminga, Philipp Ramit, Raphael Luangi, Raphael Ngunaqa, Raphael Nuavet, Rebecca Savirian, Rita Salap, Robert Vaka, Roberta Nakai, Rose Ngusurlki, Rose Boni, Sara Puatbum, Scolastica Karikmetki, Selina Qiuaik, Susan Sakalkal, Theresia Tamian, Theresia Kurukpet, Toni Alin, Utilia Avitki, and Vincent Depguasdarik

For their warm hospitality and generosity, I would like to thank Ludwina and James Tapele and their family. I gratefully remember the support of their deceased son Junior Danang.

I would like to thank the FMI (Filia Maria Immaculata) Sisters, especially Sr Wilhelmina Sundu for allowing me to stay in the Raunsepna-convent, and my house mates Sr Goretty Kuikui and Sr Roselyne Tarur for their care, hospitality, curiosity and humour.

For their hospitality and generosity, I would like to thank Joana Pascan and her family; Dorothy and Patrick Alvin; Emma and Thomas; Rose; Sheila and Jefferson Marampau.

I acknowledge the Volkswagen-Stiftung making this research possible through generous funding, and the a.r.t.e.s. Graduate School Cologne and ANU Press for funding support.

For this work, I was so lucky to become part of the Department of Linguistics at the University of Cologne. Numerous people there offered their support, guidance and friendship, for which I am incredibly grateful.

Especially, I want express my deepest gratitude to the world's best supervisor, my mentor Birgit Hellwig, for having me on the bridge, my second supervisor Nikolaus Himmelmann for his valuable comments, and for telling me to stop splitting hairs (or intonation units), and Elena Lieven from the University of Manchester for her willingness to engage with my work, the long travel she took on to do so and her insightful feedback.

I am deeply grateful to Carmen Dawuda for her tremendous support, be it on the other side of the corridor, office table or world; Steffen Reetz for sharing this journey with me; Lena Wolberg for her wizardry in overcoming bureaucratic obstacles; Sonja Eisenbeiss for her expertise and passion, and for her generosity in sharing these with me; Christoph Bracks for taking the time to truly engage with my ideas (and for tolerating my reactions to his comments); Aung Si for believing in me and for literally hundreds of commas; Ivan Kapitonov for providing stylistic advice; Gabriele Schwiertz for sharing her knowledge about phonetic analysis; Felix Rau and Volker Unterladstetter for sharing their LaTeX-skills; Sonja Riesberg for sharing her experience and insights; and Melanie Schippling, Lena Pointner and Miyuki Hennings for the numerous times they supported my linguistic analyses with their Qaqet skills and experience.

I want to thank Christian Lehmann for the dedicated training I received, and for prompting my mood of determination.

For the kind support I received in the publication of this work I want to thank Bethwyn Evans, Bruno Olsson and Angela Terrill.

I would like to thank my friends Agnes, Julia, Julian, Oliver and Susi for their vivid interest, their brilliant thoughts and the countless occasions they encouraged me.

I am deeply grateful to my parents for their unconditional love, trust and support.

Danke für Wurzeln und Flügel.

Finally, I want to thank my husband Patrick for his company, his patience, and his support and care.

Amatlungena!

Part I: Setting the scene

1
Introduction

1.1 Overview

Studying the linguistic environment of young learners is an indispensable key to the understanding of child language acquisition. The language children hear is the most important source of information they have to acquire a linguistic system. They have to connect form, meaning and diverse levels of interaction and identify the relevant cues that guide them in this process. The linguistic matter that surrounds them is one of the various forces spurring this development.

The study of child-directed speech (CDS) furthermore offers valuable insights into adult language (e.g. adult speakers' metalinguistic knowledge, as reflected in corrections of young children; Hellwig & Jung 2020) and processes of language shift (e.g. the exact processes involved in the interruption of intergenerational transfer of a language; Grenoble & Whaley 2006). We must understand processes of language shift to deal successfully with the rising loss of languages around the world. While small, marginalised language communities often find themselves confronted with the loss of their identity, linguists see the empirical base of their theories disappear (Pye 2020). The goals of these two groups do not always overlap but both could mutually benefit from responsibly conducted language documentation that includes child language and child-directed language. Currently, there are acquisition studies for about 1–2 per cent of the world's languages, and even this sample largely consists of Indo-European languages (Stoll 2015: 114). These languages not only have comparatively unusual linguistic features (Stoll 2015), but they are also mostly spoken in so-called WEIRD[1] (Western, educated, industrialised, rich, democratic), that is, hegemonic societies. These have been found to differ substantially from the majority of communities around the world on various dimensions of social description (Henrich et al. 2010). Thus, current theories of language development are based on a sample biased towards a rather atypical part of the global population:

> The vast majority of the world's languages are spoken by small populations that have fewer than a million speakers, lack socio-economic power, typically are not literate, and do not share Western cultural presuppositions. (Anand et al. 2011: 2)

Especially in rural, subsistence-based societies, the language environments of children differ substantially from Western, urban settings (Lieven & Stoll 2009). This variation in setting is reflected in the input of young language learners. Yet, children from all linguistic backgrounds typically acquire a language at roughly the same pace, following similar timetables (Casillas et al. 2020a, 2020b). In order to gain a full picture of how they achieve this, we must carefully examine the relationship between the many factors relevant to child language development in diverse contexts.

Rowe and Snow (2020) recently proposed three dimensions to analyse input to children: interactive features, linguistic features and conceptual features. They review a large amount of literature that proves that features belonging to each of these domains are helpful for child language acquisition. However, they equally predict that these features will vary between languages, cultures and other factors. Over the last few years, the study of child language development in small-scale societies has grown, providing indispensable contributions to the central questions of the field. However, much of this research focuses on the cultural context of language acquisition and the amount of language input. Nevertheless, our knowledge of the structural variation in children's input is still rather limited (Pye 2020; Hellwig & Jung 2020; Vaughan et al. 2015). The relationship between language by and with children is what ultimately influences theories of language learning. Yet, as Hellwig and Jung (2020: 208) state, 'this can only be the second step, necessitating dedicated studies later on. A first step would be to map cross-linguistic variation'.

---

1   The use of the term *educated* in this acronym is problematic. There are many other forms of education besides the formalised education intended here. If I continue to use it nevertheless, this does not mean that I want to devalue any form or construction of knowledge besides the institutionalised one.

The present work aims to push the limits a bit further by describing the register of child-directed speech in Qaqet (Baining). Spoken by about 10,000 people (Hellwig 2019: 1), Qaqet is a non-Austronesian language of the Baining Mountains of East New Britain Province, Papua New Guinea (see Figure 1.1). I collected the data for this study in Raunsepna, a remote village where people largely carry out subsistence farming, while also cultivating some cash crops. Children acquire Qaqet as their first and dominant language, followed by the national languages Tok Pisin and English. The central topic of this work is a direct comparison of language directed at adults and language directed at children (24–60 months). My findings are supplemented by a description of the socio-cultural context of children's language socialisation.

Where evident, I will describe how those factors interact with the language use evident in the comparative study. Moreover, I will attempt to make suggestions with regard to the function of the relevant features in reference to previous research.

In Section 1.2 I will outline the theoretical assumptions underlying my investigation, while referring to previous research on language directed at children.

1.2 Child-directed speech

This work draws on the assumption that input and interaction are the driving forces behind child language acquisition, a position central to the functionalist or usage-based approach to language acquisition.

In this section, I will illustrate the background of the current debates on CDS. The central topic is the effect of CDS on child language acquisition, connected to its universality and complicated by the immense amount of variation found in communities around the world.

Functionalism is one of two major, but conflicting, theoretical approaches to language acquisition. The other, nativism, assumes that children are born with knowledge about a certain number of abstract rules and principles that are universally shared by all languages in the world (Chomsky 1965, 1981). This theory arose as a reaction to the logical problem that children hear only a finite number of sentences but are able to produce an infinite number of utterances nevertheless.

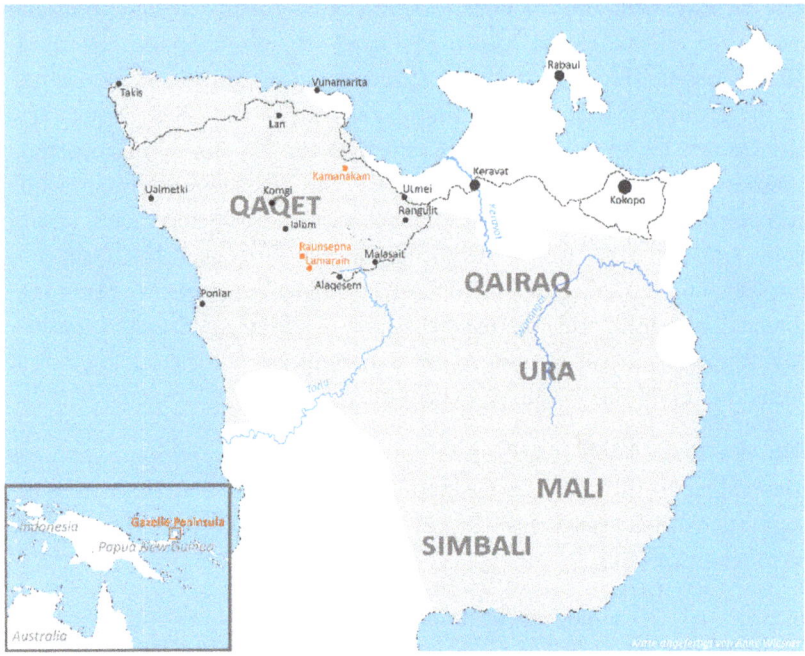

Figure 1.1: The Gazelle Peninsula in Papua New Guinea.
Source: Anne Wiesner, with permission.

Children's language input has been described as 'impoverished' (Chomsky 1965), further disqualifying its relevance for language acquisition. In reaction to this problem, nativist theories predict that, based on the very small number of sentences children hear, they would only have to activate the relevant features for their language in their innate grammar.

Piaget (1957) argued that there was no acquisition device necessary but, on the contrary, general cognitive learning mechanisms would be sufficient in order to acquire a language. Bruner (1974) and Vygotsky (1978) emphasised the role of interaction and social learning in this process. The 'motherese-hypothesis' (Snow 1972; Snow & Ferguson 1977; Nelson 1977) assumed that a specifically tailored input is the most important factor in language acquisition. These works led to functionalist or usage-based accounts of language acquisition (Tomasello 2003; Lieven & Tomasello 2008; Tomasello 2009; Ambridge & Lieven 2013). These propose that 'children's language acquisition is driven by – and hence cannot be explained without reference to – their desire to use language to perform communicative functions' (Lieven & Stoll 2013: 3). Basic cognitive abilities of children, mostly their intention-reading skills and their ability to identify patterns, enable them to identify form-function mappings in language (Tomasello 2003). For instance, joint attention, that is, when a child focuses their attention on the same shared conceptual ground as their conversational partner, can help the child identify the goals of their conversational partner and draw conclusions about the functions of the constructions they hear (Tomasello 2009).

While initially much emphasis was laid on children's language input, the children's own role in this process was never neglected:

> Language acquisition is the result of a process of interaction between mother and child which begins early in infancy, to which the child makes as important a contribution as the mother, and which is crucial to cognitive and emotional development as well as to language acquisition. (Snow 1977a)

However, later, following the ideas of Bruner (1985), the active role of children in the process of language acquisition received more attention (Gallaway & Richards 1994; Nelson 1996, 2007; de León Pasquel 2011). In the current work, I assume that the interaction between caregivers and children is of central importance in order to understand the nature of the language directed towards children. What children hear differs on various linguistic levels from the language directed at adults (Snow & Ferguson 1977; Gallaway & Richards 1994). CDS is shorter, clearer, less complex and more grammatical than adult-directed speech (ADS). It contains fewer hesitations, more imperatives and questions, its intonation patterns are exaggerated, and it is more repetitive than ADS. The vocabulary is restricted, containing reference mostly to the here and now, and less diverse than adult-directed speech.[2]

When adults speak with young children, many of these features figure prominently in their language but they disappear as the child matures (Phillips 1973; Harkness 1977), a process referred to as finetuning (Snow 1996).[3]

---

2 Summaries of the features of CDS are to be found in Snow (1972), Snow and Ferguson (1977), Gallaway and Richards (1994), O'Grady (2005), Lieven and Stoll (2009), Saxton (2009) and Vaughan et al. (2015). The detailed findings of previous research on the relevant features of CDS (Section 1.5) are presented in the respective sections.
3 This does not mean, however, that caregivers modulate their speech consciously to provide adapted language lessons for their children.

There is broad evidence that several features of CDS support language acquisition in various ways (Richards & Gallaway 1994). Reduced complexity (e.g. of utterances, see Chapter 4) facilitates comprehension by minimising the processing effort and necessary concentration span (Newport et al. 1977). Explicit prompts to listen, content questions, variation sets and a higher fundamental frequency (Warren-Leubecker & Bohannon 1984) serve to attract and direct children's attention: focusing on the 'relevant aspects of the context is a necessary condition for the acquisition of a language and for successful communication' (Richards & Gallaway 1994: 263). Prosodic features (see Chapter 6) such as an exaggerated frequency range and hesitations potentially facilitate identification of the boundaries of words and phrases, given that the relevant modifications often occur at salient positions in the sentence (Richards & Gallaway 1994; Snow 1972; Jones & Meakins 2013).

Negative evidence such as recasts (target-like repetitions of the children's non target-like utterances) provide the child with useful information regarding the acceptability of her utterance (Cross 1977; Hoff-Ginsberg & Shatz 1982; Barnes et al. 1983; Farrar 1990; Saxton 1997). Due to their proximity (both within the sentence and also semantically) to the utterance they refer to, recasts are also highly intelligible (Barnes et al. 1983; Saxton 1997).

As a consequence of this discovery, early research hypothesised that CDS was necessary for language acquisition, and therefore universal by definition (Snow & Ferguson 1977). However, the interplay of diverse factors turned out to be more complex than assumed. I illustrate this by referencing research on the effect of disfluencies on comprehension:

> Disfluencies provide neither semantic nor syntactic information; as a matter of fact, disfluencies provide the child with 'false' information [...] Intuitively, therefore, it would seem that disfluent speech should be hard for young children to process and we might expect that speech addressed to young children would be relatively free of disfluency. (Broen 1972: 4)[4]

This view has been challenged by recent developments providing evidence that certain types of disfluencies tend to occur ahead of 'difficult linguistic material' (Clark & Fox Tree 2002; Owens et al. 2018; Thacker et al. 2018: 5). Hesitation particles such as *uh* or *uhm* in English, for

---

4   Ellipsis that appear in square brackets indicate that the author has removed unnecessary text from a quote; ellipsis that appear without square brackets are as they appear in the original quoted text.

example, often occur before words introducing new discourse referents or referring to infrequent ones (Nilsson Björkenstam et al. 2013). Even toddlers of 28–32 months of age 'use disfluencies online to compute expectations about the speaker's referential intentions' (Kidd et al. 2011: 13). Hesitations, therefore, are not necessarily hard to process, and fewer hesitations are not necessarily beneficial for comprehension.

If CDS was a necessary condition for language acquisition, we would expect it to be universal. Due to a bias towards WEIRD languages (see Section 1.1), early research did not consider variations between different languages. Evidence for this variation was provided by scholars from the paradigm of language socialisation (Ochs & Schieffelin 1984; Schieffelin & Ochs 1986), who not only demonstrated that the learning environments of children differ extensively around the world, but that this variation crucially affects language directed towards children (CDS).

Neither in Samoa (Ochs 1988) nor among the Kaluli of Papua New Guinea (Schieffelin 1990) was a register of child-directed speech discovered. On the contrary, children in both communities receive little direct input and only rarely experience dyadic or coordinated joint attention.[5] Both Schieffelin and Ochs demonstrated how the ideologies held within those communities towards children and child language acquisition were responsible for these linguistic practices. Similar evidence has since been reported for many children from non-industrial societies. The complex and varying relationships between socio-economic factors, caregiving-styles, parental beliefs and actual language practice are the topic of Chapter 2. The amount of variation between language environments is substantial and far from being sufficiently explored.

Still, in recent years, there have been advances in mapping this diversity, and drawing the relevant conclusions concerning the mechanisms of child language acquisition. While in many societies, children receive only very little directed speech, it is probable that all societies have their own special ways of interacting with children; however, different languages yield 'different ranges of modifications' (Gallaway & Richards 1994: 257).

In many languages, the mean fundamental frequency is higher in CDS than in ADS. Bryant and Barrett (2007) show that adult Shuar hunter horticulturalists from Amazonian Ecuador can discriminate between

---

5   Dyadic joint attention happens between two people, while coordinated joint attention happens when two people interact together with a concrete object.

English ADS and CDS when listening to samples, and are better at inferring speaker intentions from the CDS-samples. These findings were replicated with adults from the Turkana society in northwestern Kenya (Bryant et al. 2012), suggesting that the subjects know the relevant registers from their own languages. Yet, Pye (1986a), for K'iche' Maya, and Defina (2020), for the Australian language Pitjantjatjara, both report the mean fundamental frequency to be the same in CDS, and occasionally even lower than in ADS. With regard to utterance type, Rowe (2008) and Hoff-Ginsberg and Shatz (1982) found that a great prevalence of questions is not only typical for CDS (in WEIRD languages), but is also associated with growth in the vocabulary of children. However, Pye (1986a) reports that K'iche' CDS contained even fewer questions than ADS. Instead, he found a large number of imperatives. Vogt et al. (2015) report equally high amounts of imperatives for Changana in a rural community in Mozambique, but much less in a nearby urban community.

From these few instances of possible variation, the following question emerges: how do these input characteristics, which are so different from those that have been reported to be salient, interact with children's language acquisition? Recent research has addressed the effect of CDS on vocabulary size in communities where children receive little directed input. As children in many societies only receive minimal directed input, it seems likely that they are able to learn from overheard speech. The results, though, are contradictory. Shneidman and Goldin-Meadow (2012) found that Yucatec Mayan children did not profit from overheard speech despite receiving little directed speech. Rural children in Mozambique (Mastin & Vogt 2015), however, apparently learned new words from watching the actions of others.

Yet in both groups—Mayan children and children in Mozambique—the total amount of language directly addressed to them correlated with vocabulary growth. This highlights the central importance of CDS for language acquisition and the urgent need to document its manifold faces.

1.3 Qaqet Baining

1.3.1 The Qaqet language

Qaqet is a non-Austronesian language and a member of the Baining language family that consists furthermore of the distinct languages Mali, Simbali, Kairak, Uramot and Makolkol (Stebbins 2009). The Baining people are very likely the original inhabitants of the Gazelle Peninsula (Stebbins 2009). All of the languages are minority languages while Makolkol is possibly even extinct (Hellwig 2019). They are associated with the geographically defined East Papuan languages, a group of 25 non-Austronesian languages spoken in Island Melanesia (Hellwig 2019). For a full description of Qaqet grammar, see Hellwig (2019).

In accessible coastal regions, Qaqet people live together with people from various ethnolinguistic backgrounds. Thus, Tok Pisin—their lingua franca—is taking over rapidly in many domains and Qaqet is becoming increasingly marginalised (Hellwig 2019). In remote inland villages, however, the situation is different. Marley (2013) finds that few non-Qaqet live in Raunsepna; these include several non-Qaqet spouses who live with their Qaqet families, but mainly mission staff who stay only temporarily. As such, there is little necessity for the use of Tok Pisin (Marley 2013). As a consequence, Qaqet is spoken regularly in all domains of daily life, and acquired as a first language by children, resulting in a fairly stable language situation.

1.3.2 Colonial history

During the last centuries, the Qaqet Baining experienced marginalisation and violence from various actors. Near the end of the eighteenth century, the Tolai, the dominant ethnic group in East New Britain nowadays, arrived from New Ireland (Stebbins 2009). From the very beginning, the relationship between the two groups was hostile. Baining people suffered from raids and enslavement by the invaders (Fajans 1997: 33f). The Tolai considered themselves superior and conveyed their negative image of the Baining people to the German missionaries (Hiery 2007).

Colonialists then took Baining land, forcing the Baining to live in centralised settlements and work for others on their own heritage land (Fajans 1997: 37ff). During the Great War, when Australians took colonial leadership from Germany, influenza and other epidemics diminished the population considerably. During World War II, Japanese occupiers killed and tortured Bainings and destroyed their crops (Fajans 1997: 40ff). By the 1950s, coastal Baining populations had been so diminished that they were called a 'dying people' (Hiery 2007: 8), a prediction that fortunately has not come true.

The mountainous inland regions of the island were not visited by missionaries until 1939, the first of whom only returned in 1951 (Hiery 2007). At that time, Catholic missionaries established the mission centre at Raunsepna. They built a hospital, a school and a road, which was however destroyed by torrential rains in the early nineties.

Even today, Baining people experience marginalisation from neighbouring groups (Dickhardt 2009; Rohatynskyj 2001; Hiery 2007). Moreover, with globalisation, the land grabbing practices of logging and palm oil companies further threaten their lives and livelihoods as self-sufficient people who exclusively rely on their own land.

1.3.3 Previous research

Early work on the Qaqet language dates back to the beginning of the twentieth century. The first grammar was published by Rascher (Missionarii Sacratissimi Cordis, MSC), a missionary who lived for years among the Northern Qaqet (Rascher 1904). Further notes on the language can be found in Parkinson (1907) and Schmidt (1905), followed by word lists (Stehlin 1905/1906; Volmer 1926) and a grammar sketch (Volmer 1928). There is a collection of edited narratives (Bley 1914). Later, missionaries from the Summer Institute of Linguistics (SIL) published a phonological sketch (Parker & Parker 1974) and a grammar sketch (Parker & Parker 1977). The linguistic analyses in the present study are based on the extended grammar by Hellwig (2019).

For the sociolinguistic background, this work draws on an MA thesis about language use among the Qaqet in Raunsepna (Marley 2013) and on work by Hellwig (2020) and Hellwig and Jung (2020). The latter attests the presence of variation sets in CDS in Raunsepna, which is one of the typical features of CDS (see Section 1.2). Likewise, work on language attitudes in the Baining communities of Mali (Stebbins 2004) and Uramot (Stanton 2007) has informed the present study.

The Qaqet have received a considerable amount of anthropological interest (Parkinson 1907; Burger 1913; Rascher 1909; Laufer 1946–49, 1959; Hesse & Aerts 1982; Hesse 2007; Rohatynskyj 2000, 2001; Fajans 1983, 1985, 1993; Dickhardt 2012). Their colonial history is described in detail by Hiery (2007). For the anthropological aspects in the present study, two publications are of special importance. Dickhardt (2009) studied the concept of morality among the Qaqet, based on several field stays in Raunsepna between 2002 and 2006. He provides detailed descriptions of the economic background and moral principles in the village. Fajans (1997) based her ethnography of the Qaqet Baining on fieldwork conducted in the 1970s in two villages. Among other topics, she also provides a detailed analysis of Baining child care practices. A central point in her description is her claim that 'child culture' is scarce among the Baining, and play is devalued by adults:

> The Baining [...] regard children's play as the antithesis of proper social activity [...] This is why, although Baining children are not treated harshly, the Baining suppress spontaneous play by children. (Fajans 1997: 168)

Further, Fajans argues that 'a society that fixates on work and suppresses play can become (at least through our eyes) a dull society' (1997: 7). Lattas (2020) describes how this portrayal of the Baining as a dull society without social structure or even gossip has been received and used in various media channels despite the protests of other researchers who have worked with them. He criticises Fajans's 'depolitical understanding of fieldwork problems' (Lattas 2020: 103), which does not take into consideration that the Baining were deliberately avoiding being studied, an interpretation he shares with Dickhardt (2009: 132):

> this habitus is not a disposition of shyness and dullness, but rather an attitude of intentional distancing and resistance against inappropriate arrogation, in an effort to retain their own autonomy.[6]

Anthropological research reproduced the marginalisation that the Baining had experienced from various outsiders by establishing an image of a non-playful, dull culture (Lattas 2020). With the progress of digitisation and the ubiquity of the internet, this image arrived on the first smartphones in Baining villages, raising awareness of the image reproduced among anthropologists and thereby reviving yet again structures that should long have been overcome.

---

6   Translation by author. Original: *so erscheint dieser Habitus weniger ein Habitus der Scheu und Stumpfheit als vielmehr ein Habitus gewollter Distanzierung und Widerständigkeit gegen als unangemessen erachtete autoritäre Anmaßung im Bemühen darum, die eigene Autonomie zu erhalten.*

1.3.4 The community: Raunsepna

Figure 1.2: The valley of Raunsepna, seen from the gardens in the mountains.
Source: Photograph by the author.

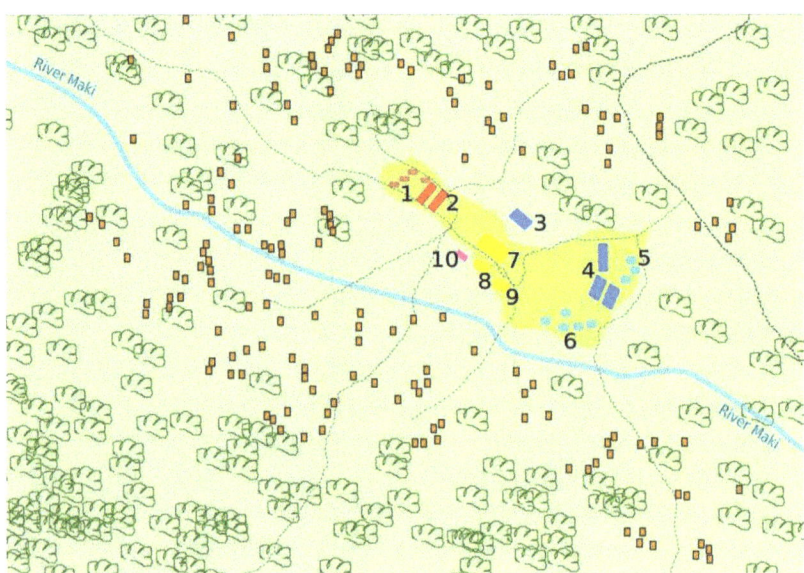

Figure 1.3: Map of the Raunsepna mission centre today.
Note: Scattered brown squares: villagers' homes; yellow area = mission centre; 1 = nurses' homes; 2 = hospital; 3 = elementary school building; 4 = primary school buildings; 5 and 6 = teachers' homes; 7 = church; 8 = convent; 9 = priest's house; 10 = linguists' work house.
Source: Map produced by the author.

1. INTRODUCTION

Raunsepna (see Figure 1.2) is a remote village in the Baining Mountains (see Figure 1.1) that consists of four hamlets (see map in Figure 1.3). The village is inhabited by approximately 1,300 people (Dickhardt 2009) who live primarily from subsistence gardening supplemented by a cash crop economy. The basic household unit consists of a married couple and their unmarried children.[7]

According to Dickhardt (2009: 140), most households cultivate three to four subsistence gardens, sized 0.25–0.5 hectares. Some of these gardens are located close to the village centre, while others are only accessible after several hours of walking. The most important staple foods from the garden are taro and Singapore taro, supplemented by a large variety of leafy greens. There are also several other crops like cassava, sweet potatoes, corn and wild sugarcane. This diet is enriched by some hunting (e.g. of birds, wallabies) and occasionally by meat from pigs and chickens.

Major cash crops today are peanuts, which are grown in the mountains close to the village and alongside the road to Malasait (see Figure 1.1), and cocoa and copra, which are cultivated in plots of land close to the coast referred to as 'blocks'. For most families, cash crops are their only source of monetary income; the harvest is mostly sold to distributors in the markets of Kerevat and Kokopo.

Due to the distribution of the gardens and blocks over a large area, most families live a highly mobile lifestyle with different members of the family regularly spending extended periods of time in temporary houses close to the various areas under cultivation.

Despite this, the houses close to the village centre of Raunsepna (see Figure 1.3) are considered the primary home by most families from Raunsepna (Dickhardt 2009). The so-called *station* at the centre of the village provides services run by the Catholic church such as a health post, a school (elementary and primary) and a convent. Qaqet from all over the region regularly visit Raunsepna for these services. Occasionally, children from other villages are left semi-permanently with their relatives in Raunsepna to attend school.

---

7   Older relatives occasionally dwell with their family if they need support, but usually, even single elders or widows choose to stay in their own houses, see Dickhardt (2009: 140).

1.4 Database and methods

In language acquisition research, a combination of different types of data are considered a best-practice-approach (Kelly & Nordlinger 2014). Hellwig (2020: 37) describes the challenges posed by the application of certain methodologies in non-Western settings far from lab conditions:

> On the one hand, there is a need to document characteristic speech practices—in their own right, and as instances of alternative ways of socializing children into narrating stories. And, on the other hand, there is a need to follow prescribed methodologies that arose in Western contexts—methodologies that were developed for good reasons, and that make the collected data comparable cross-linguistically.

In the present study, different data types and methods have been used to describe the register of CDS in Qaqet and compare it to Qaqet ADS.[8] In this section, the choice of each method will be explained with regard to its advantages and disadvantages for the actual purpose. Descriptions of the methods are found in the relevant chapters. All the data were collected during three extended field stays in 2015 (two months), 2016 (seven months) and 2017 (two months).

This study mainly draws on staged data from a narrative study using the Pear Film (Chafe 1980) as a stimulus (see Section 3.1 for a full description). This method has the benefit of allowing many aspects of the situation to be controlled by the researcher. It enabled me to choose the participants and the content of the communicative event. Each adult participant was asked to produce two versions of the same story, one directed at a child, and one at an adult.

In this way, two comparable subcorpora were created. These systematically compared differences between the two data sets can thus be attributed to differences between the two registers in Qaqet, namely ADS vs CDS.

Reference to examples from the staged corpus will be made by specifying the text name, for example, Pear plus the narrator's three letter speaker code (e.g. ARL) and an A for 'adult' and a P for 'child' (*pikinini* 'child' in

---

8 The present work is a description of the register of CDS in Qaqet. No production data from children are included, hence no conclusions regarding the effects of input on child language development will be made.

Tok Pisin), for example, PearAMTP for the Pear Story narrated by AMT to a child. Additionally, the example's running number in the specific text is given. The name of the example source is given following the free translation. The corpus has been analysed quantitatively for features reported by previous research as typical of CDS in other languages. With 10 data sets for comparison (consisting of an ADS- and a CDS-version of the narration), the present study draws on a relatively small sample. Therefore, all statistical tests used are non-parametric, which is the best choice if tests for a normal distribution are impossible due to small sample sizes. In addition to the quantitative comparisons, discourse-analytical methods have been applied to investigate interactional patterns.

Despite their benefits for comparability, staged data are susceptible to effects of the stimulus and the recording situation (see Section 3.1 for details on challenges encountered in the current study), and therefore do not produce naturalistic outcomes. Accordingly, the outcomes have to be compared to other data types. The present study draws on four more data types: interviews, participant observation, entire-day-data (i.e. audio-recordings of children's language environment) and longitudinal data.

I conducted 22 interviews with 36 participants about their attitudes towards child care, child language and language in general (a detailed description of the methodology is given in Section 2.2). The references for examples from the interviews are specified following their free translation, consisting of 'Int' for the text-type 'Interview' and the speaker codes of those who participated in the interview.

In order to assess language attitudes in a given community, questionnaires or interviews are usually employed. As direct techniques, 'interviews or questionnaires typically measure consciously and deliberately constructed and expressed attitudes' (Speelman et al. 2013: 84). Interviewees may decide on their own what information they are willing to share. Instead of regarding this as a weakness of the method, this quality of direct techniques could also be appreciated as preserving the autonomy of the subjects.

The decision to conduct interviews instead of using questionnaires was motivated by insights from previous research. Agheyisi and Fishman (1970) remark that 'the research interview can be particularly effective for attitude assessment, especially when used to complement the observational method' (Agheyisi & Fishman 1970: 151). A further benefit they report is that interviews, as opposed to formalised questionnaires, allow the researcher to react in a flexible manner to the moods of the interviewee and adapt the method, if necessary. For the present study I benefitted not only from the results, but also from the methodological experience gained from previous research on attitudes conducted in Raunsepna: Marley (2013) reported difficulties with questionnaires, mostly due to the low familiarity of the participants with the method, while group interviews worked well. Hence, I decided to conduct interviews with at least two people present, allowing for the possibility for the interviewees discuss the answers collaboratively.

Despite the aforementioned benefits of direct techniques for the autonomy of subjects, there are some disadvantages. Haggan (2002), assessing beliefs about the use of CDS among Kuwaiti adults, demonstrated that interviews do not capture the true language behaviour of a community. Reported behaviour and actual behaviour vastly differed. Thus, in addition to the interviews, I employed other methods to collect data on the actual language behaviour of people in contact with children.

For this purpose, I employed two methods. First, I took the results from participant observation into account: primarily in Chapter 2, but occasionally in the other chapters of this work. Participant observation as a method is based on interpretation (Milroy & Gordon 2003): all impressions are filtered through the lens of the researcher's own background. However, regular interaction with the community on a day-to-day-basis allowed me to familiarise myself with many people, with their customs and their thoughts. Thereby, I gained insights that otherwise might have been ignored, as described by Eckert (2004). In personal encounters, participants are usually more open and relaxed than when being recorded. Moreover, the mutual trust built in regular personal encounters is helpful for most other methods of data collection with the community. Still, data from participant observation can usually not be evaluated quantitatively. In order to gain data on the amount of speech children hear in the course of the day, I decided to supplement the data from participant observation with naturalistic audio recordings.

I audio-recorded four children's actual language environments on several days to test for the amount and the source of their input. In the present work, these data have been incorporated to supplement the findings from the interviews with regard to the language environment. The use of audio data instead of videos was originally intended to make the method less obtrusive. Still, in practice, the nature of these data turned out to be hard to process due to the missing video. Moreover, only a small part of the data collected could be used for analysis. Still, the recordings of children's entire days allow for a preliminary estimation of the amount of input and the types of activities that are typical for a child's linguistic environment.

Throughout the study, occasional reference will be made to the longitudinal corpus constructed by our research team[9] since 2014 (Hellwig et al. 2014–19). The corpus comprises weekly, hour-long video-recordings of children from nine families, four of these from Raunsepna and five from coastal Kamanakam, resulting in a corpus of more than 250 hours of recorded spontaneous interactions. For the present study, only the data from the families dwelling in Raunsepna have been used. The benefit of these longitudinal data is that they are more naturalistic than staged data, and allow for insights into the development of children. Unfortunately, the construction of longitudinal corpora is an extremely time-consuming effort. These longitudinal data are thus not yet in a state that allows for systematic data extraction. Therefore, only preliminary insights will be reported, mainly to complement the entire-day-data in Chapter 2. First impressions will be reported to allow for estimations about the occurrence of certain observations in naturalistic rather than staged contexts. Such preliminaries are incorporated to build hypotheses that may be tested by future research.

Once in a state to allow for systematic tests, the longitudinal corpus will enable us to test hypotheses derived from the data on which the present study is based.

All the data have been archived with the Language Archive Cologne.[10] Due to the sensitive nature of data that includes children, access is restricted. During fieldwork, I discussed access rights and ownership of data in detail with all the participants to obtain informed consent.

If researchers aim to study a certain culture, they must not only keep in mind the history of the culture in question but also their own background. All research on culture is shaped by the researchers' beliefs and values (Errington 2008: 5). Ascribing certain patterns to a whole culture or language community is always a delicate matter, especially as these patterns may be driven by unconscious beliefs of how things should be.

---

9   Documenting Child Language: The Qaqet Baining of Papua New Guinea. Funded by the Volkswagen Foundation's Lichtenberg Program.
10 Hellwig, Birgit, Carmen Dawuda, Henrike Frye & Steffen Reetz. 2014–19. *Qaqet corpus*.

Early colonial anthropology is often very clearly based on the assumption of the superiority of the researchers' own culture and therefore promotes colonial interests (Errington 2008: 12). However, while these assumptions may be less obvious in today's research, the distribution of power between the studied and the studying unfortunately has not changed much.

The present work is also based on a profound imbalance in the relationship between the researcher and the participants. While I have the ability to travel and to do research, this is not the case for the people with whom I am working in Raunsepna. My observations and interpretations are just as mediated by my attitudes as everyone else's.

1.5 Outlook

This monograph is divided into two parts. Part I, consisting of this chapter and the following one, lays the foundation for Part II. In Chapter 2, I investigate the language environment of children in Raunsepna. With regard to the amount of language, I determine if it is comparable to the amount that children in similar settings receive. For beliefs about child language acquisition, I present interview results that connect to patterns found in actual language practice. Additionally, I offer new evidence on child play among the Qaqet. The chapter contextualises the staged data presented in Part II, where the results of seven empirical substudies are presented, each presenting my investigation of single features that are known to vary between CDS and ADS in other languages. In Chapter 3, I introduce the Qaqet Pear corpus. Chapters 4 to 7 are dedicated to a quantitative comparison of ADS and CDS. Additionally, I assess potential benefits for children of the type of input found in the data, based on previous research on the effect of such input. While this is also true for Chapters 8 and 9, I concentrate on the modifications found in CDS, as there are no instances of the relevant phenomena in the ADS corpus.

2
The language environment

This chapter is designed to contextualise the comparative study on the features of CDS in Part II. In Section 2.1, the connections between children's linguistic input and their caregivers' attitudes towards caregiving, learning and the language itself will be explored. In Section 2.2, I present the results from interviews with adults in Raunsepna concerning those attitudes.[1] The participants recount diverse aspects of child rearing, language and child language acquisition. Their attitudes are then compared to previous research on Baining people and other non-WEIRD societies. I supplement this discussion with a presentation of results from a pilot study I conducted on the amount of speech Qaqet children receive from different interlocutors (Section 2.3). Additionally, I employ preliminary insights from the longitudinal data (see Section 1.4) to integrate the results from Section 2.3. The insights from both types of data are enhanced by data from participant observation in Raunsepna.

2.1 Child rearing practices and frameworks of interaction

The socio-economic environment in which children grow up influences what they are expected to learn. Keller (2007, 2012) describes three prototypical types of communities and the way the socio-economic

---
1 The terms *attitudes* and *ideologies* will be used synonymously referring to shared or individual sets of beliefs. For further discussion and differentiation see Dyers and Abongdia (2010) and Kroskrity (2004).

environment relates to the developmental trajectories of children growing up in these societies: Western urban, non-Western urban and non-Western rural societies.[2]

In prototypical Western, urban societies (corresponding largely to WEIRD or post-industrial societies), children are primarily expected to perform at school. The amount of formal education is typically high, and becoming a successful member of society is mediated by individual psychological autonomy: children are expected to know about their own inner states and to express them. Verbal communication is the most important means to meet these expectations. This results not only in a high amount of CDS, but also in frequent triadic joint attention, much face-to-face-interaction (Keller 2012; Mastin & Vogt 2015) and a high number of cognitive intentions in child-directed speech (Mastin & Vogt 2015; Vogt et al. 2015: 349). Cognitive intentions are, for example, goals to stimulate children's language development or, more broadly, their understanding and expression of their environment (Mastin & Vogt 2015: 345).

In many places, in order to become a successful member of society, children must become productive members of their subsistence-based community. This primarily entails taking on a variety of household duties from early on, like cleaning the house, fetching water or wood and caring for younger siblings (Lancy 2008). Children's motor independence is fostered, for example, by having them retrieve objects (Mastin & Vogt 2015). The leading principle of socialisation is communal action autonomy:

> Children are expected to be helpers who can act in self-determined and self-responsible ways with a focus on the functioning and wellbeing of the social unit. (Keller 2012: 15)

In such communities, children typically receive a small amount of CDS and much of their linguistic input takes the form of directives. Multiparty settings are the norm, and children spend a significant part of the day in the company of other children.[3] Despite all differences, however, the broad developmental milestones are similar across cultures (Casillas et al. 2020a).

---

2 For illustration, in the present section I only describe the first and the last. The non-Western, urban societies lie somewhere in between these two poles.
3 This was described by Schieffelin (1990) for the Kaluli in Papua New Guinea, Ochs (1988) for Samoans in Western Samoa, Kulick (1992) for the Gapuners in Papua New Guinea, Bavin (1992) for Warlpiri in Australia, Pye (1992) for the K'iche' Maya in Guatemala, Lieven (1994), Shneidman and Goldin-Meadow (2012) for Yucatec Mayans in Mexico, Cristia et al. (2017) for the Tsimane in Bolivia, Vogt et al. (2015) and Mastin and Vogt (2015) for rural versus urban societies in Mozambique, Casillas et al. (2020b) for Tseltal Maya, and Casillas et al. (2020a) for Rossel Islanders in Papua New Guinea.

The expectations towards children correlate with parental ethnotheories of learning (Harkness et al. 2010; Gaskins & Paradise 2010). While in Western, urban societies, there is an emphasis on explicit instruction, in small scale rural societies, children often learn through a style called guided participation:

> Children in communities that allow or promote observation of adult activities may develop largely through their own initiative, through active observation and gradually increasing participation. (Rogoff et al. 1993)

Parental beliefs about learning can have pervasive effects on the input children receive. Well-known examples from the paradigm of language socialisation are described by Kulick (1992) and Ochs and Schieffelin (1984). Kulick describes how parents' beliefs about how children acquire language became a critical factor in the loss of the vernacular. In Gapun, the village described by Kulick, villagers came to associate their vernacular Taiap with backwardness while Tok Pisin, the lingua franca of Papua New Guinea, was associated with modernity and wealth. Subsequently, Taiap was increasingly undervalued and neglected. Therefore, caregivers chose Tok Pisin when speaking to their children, who, in turn, received hardly any input in the vernacular language. Moreover, the responsibility for language acquisition was perceived to lie in the hands of children; adults did not consider themselves capable of teaching them Taiap. They felt that even if they had decided to prevent the language shift, it would be outside of their ability to change their children's course of learning. These attitudes resulted in a rapid language shift towards Tok Pisin in that community.

For the Kaluli in Papua New Guinea, Schieffelin (1990) reported that adults did not believe young children could understand language until they used it productively themselves. Similar evidence is reported by Ochs (1988) for Samoan children, where adults likewise see no necessity in teaching their children language. In both cultures, children are not considered adequate conversational partners for adults and dyadic interactions between adults and children, the former primary target of language acquisition studies, hardly occur at all. Moreover, there is no simplified register for addressing infants. These are only some examples to show how much variation there is in language ideologies and theories of learning and the degree to which they are intertwined with the language environment of children. For the Qaqet, Fajans (1997) reports that people do not think that it makes sense to talk to babies up to the age of six months.

Casillas et al. (2020a) argue that ideologies may not be the most important factor with regard to the amount and form of input children receive. Rossel Islanders see their children as adequate communicative partners, yet the amount of language used with children is comparable to what previous studies found for other rural small-scale societies. Thus, they argue that situational factors are at the root of comparable input rates in subsistence-based societies. Not ideologies, but rather the number of speakers present and the activities performed explained peak times of input for Rossel Island children. Those factors will be addressed in Section 2.3 for the Qaqet in Raunsepna.

In the following I will show that in terms of the community types described by Keller (2007), Raunsepna can be described as a fairly typical rural, non-Western community. People live by means of subsistence farming and although there is formal schooling, this has no practical relation to the future lives of many people, as most stay in the village as farmers. Moreover, school attendance is very irregular and students frequently drop out. The following analysis of attitudes will show that communal action autonomy is the main principle guiding child socialisation. The amount of input is comparable to input rates described for other small scale rural societies. Specific situational contexts as well as individual differences also play important roles. In terms of beliefs about learning, I will demonstrate that although a style of guided participation prevails, parents nevertheless consider themselves responsible for teaching their children Qaqet. I mostly make use of direct quotes obtained from the interviews to illustrate participants' attitudes.

2.2 Assessing attitudes

2.2.1 Methods and data

It is not a straightforward issue to come to know of a certain population's sets of beliefs and opinions towards one or more domains of society. In order to explore the relevant attitudes in Raunsepna, a method was developed in several steps, as presented in Table 2.1. Steps 1–4 are preparatory, and so the following discussion concentrates on the results from Step 5.

Table 2.1: Methodological steps towards an assessment of language attitudes in Raunsepna (RS).

Step	Activity	Purpose
1	Literature research	Find topics that interact with language environment of children
2	Open, unstructured interviews (not recorded)	Explore the relevance of topics in RS, find further topics
3	Coding of the interview notes	Identify salient and frequent attitudes in RS
4	Compile a list of statements as interview guideline	Summarise salient and frequent attitudes in RS
5	Semi-structured interviews (recorded)	Confirm/disconfirm the statements; elicit commentary

In the following discussion, the steps towards the final interviews are described. First (Step 1 from Table 2.1), I compiled a list of topics from the literature. I aimed for insights into spheres known to interact with children's language environment. To ensure that I targeted topics considered relevant by the villagers themselves, I conducted unstructured interviews during my preparatory stay in Raunsepna in 2015. I asked adults to tell me everything they considered important concerning children's lives, child care and language (Step 2 from Table 2.1). This resulted in 23 sessions with approximately 50 people.[4] Even during preliminary interviews, it proved challenging to talk about other people's motivations, as people were reluctant to speculate about the motivations of others, responding frequently to such questions with *mipela i no save long ol* 'we do not know about them'. This is a common attitude in Pacific societies that is referred to as the doctrine of the opacity of other minds by Robbins and Rumsey (2008) and can impact discussions on attitudes towards others' actions.

In order to create an environment as comfortable as possible for everyone (Du Bois 1980), I did not record those conversations. Instead I took notes and coded these for topic (Step 3 from Table 2.1). As a last preparatory step, I compiled a list comprising 64 statements targeting primarily four different domains (Step 2 from Table 2.1):

---

[4] Due to the open setup and because many interviews were held in people's homes or gardens to avoid pressure on the participants, people often dropped in, participated for a while and dropped out again.

- learning/chore curriculum
- playing
- respect
- (child) language.

Several topics are not covered in the following discussion though they figured prominently in the unstructured interviews: I excluded religious education, as it is associated with much Tok Pisin use (Marley 2013) and adoption, although a central practice (Fajans 1997), because it would go far beyond the scope of the present work. The domain of maintenance activities (feeding and hygiene) has been shown to elicit large amounts of speech (Glas et al. 2018) and was also identified by the participants as a peak time of verbal interaction during the day. However, the explanations in the preliminary interview were focused on how to attend to children's bodily needs rather than on details of language use. For information regarding language use during such activities, naturalistic data are presumably more informative (as a first step) than an interview-format. On the other hand, given that the data elicited for the comparison of CDS and ADS are narratives, it would have been wise to include questions concerning storytelling practices between adults and children. Fortunately, I can refer to reports by Hellwig (2020) to explore this topic.

The interplay between the topics I included and language socialisation has been described in detail in Section 2.1, so I will only briefly recall their relevance here. **The chore curriculum** consists of all those tasks 'that all boys or all girls should master by a roughly agreed upon age and carry out willingly and efficiently' (Lancy 2012a). It has similar characteristics across many subsistence-based cultures (Jensen & Gaskins 2015) and structures the everyday life of children. It reflects adults' expectations towards children, which, in turn, are responsible for the communicative styles used towards them (see Section 2.1). **Play** was included, as there have been previous reports that Baining people, unlike nearly all the other cultures in the world, do not play with their children and even suppress child play (Fajans 1997). **Attitudes towards language and learning**, as described in Section 2.1, have a direct impact on the course of language socialisation. **Respect**, one of the moral values described by Dickhardt (2009) as a leading principle of morality among the Baining, was identified by interviewees as especially relevant for child education. The full list of statements I used in the semi-structured interviews is to be found in the Appendix. To illustrate the form of those statements, some examples are presented here:

- (1) *Ol pikinini i laik bihainim ol bikpela long wok.* 'Children like to imitate adults' work.'
- (8) *Ol pikinini ol i mas lain long wok gaden.* 'Children must learn to do garden work.'
- (33) *Taim i gat visita long haus, ol pikinini noken ran nabaut na pilai.* 'If there are visitors in the house, children cannot run around and play.'

The statements were read to the participants during the structured interviews in 2017 (Step 5 from Table 2.1). Participants were informed that those statements had been made by other people from Raunsepna and that in order to make sure that they really mirrored the attitudes held within the community, I was going to ask as many people as possible to deny or confirm the relevant statements.

Of course, it is possible that people assumed I expected them to confirm the statements. Excluding interviewer-bias is a challenge for the validity of any interview (Briggs 1986: 21). In fact, there was a great deal of confirmation in the answers; hardly any statements were rejected. This may be partly due to the methodology chosen: I mostly included only those topics that had already figured prominently in the unstructured interviews. More controversial topics may not have made it into the second interview session. Furthermore, the Qaqet Baining have a consensus-oriented interaction style (Dickhardt 2009: 271ff), and therefore might be reluctant to show dissent. One good indication, however, that the interviewees did report their own thoughts or those of the community was that they often completed the statement before I could finish reading it. See the quotation below:

> **Interviewer:** *Olsem ol i harim papa na mama ol i toktok …*
> 'So, they hear their parents talk …'
> **AMM:** *… na ol i bihainim.*
> '… and they imitate.' (Int_AMM_AVD)

Altogether, 22 interviews were conducted and audio-recorded with 36 participants. All the participants who had been involved as narrators or listeners in the pear story corpus recordings, and were still available in 2017, participated in an interview. Additionally, I included every other Qaqet L1 speaker who was available. See Table 2.2 below for the details about the participants. 'PS' indicates that those participants later participated in the comparative study described later in this volume. A question mark indicates that there is no information available.

Table 2.2: Interviewees' speaker code (ID), sex, age, number of children (Chi), participation in the comparative study in Part II (PS) and formal education.

Code	No.	Sex	Birth	Chi	PS	Formal Education
CCM	1	m	1975	8	no	Catechist school
AAI	1	f	1979	8	no	Grade 6
BJS	2	f	1986	-	no	Grade 10
CLS	3	f	1981	8	no	Grade 6
BFN	3	m	1977	8	no	VT Welder
AMM	4	f	1991	3	no	Grade 8
AVD	4	m	1983	3	yes	Grade 6
EAK	5	f	1993	1	no	Grade 8
DBK	5	m	1996	1	no	Grade 8
ASQ	6	f	1981	6	no	Grade 6
DCK	6	m	1977	6	yes	Grade 6
ABD	7	f	1980	7	yes	ES teacher education)
ACP	7	m	1978	7	no	Grade 10; Short Course in Business Education
ARB	8	f	1977	3	no	Grade 6
ADK	8	m	1963	3	no	VT Carpenter
AAS	9	f	1980	5	no	VT Sewing/Cooking
ARS	10	f	1983	1	no	VT
AMW	11	m	1974	3	no	Grade 6
AME	11	f	1980	3	no	Grade 6
ARN	12	f	1982	10	no	Grade 3
BCP	12	m	1976	10	yes	Grade 6
DCM	13	m	1957	16	yes	Grade 6
AMI	13	f	1962	16	yes	Grade 6
AMT	14	f	1990	2	yes	VT Tourism
CRN	15	m	2000	0	no	2017: Grade 6
BRS	15	f	1968	7	no	Grade 6
BLN	16	f	1985	4	yes	Grade 10
APA	16	m	1982	4	no	Grade 10
AMS	17	f	1980	1	no	Grade 6
ARL	17	m	1979	6	yes	Grade 6
AML	18	f	1991	1	no	Grade 8
ACM	18	m	1975	7	no	ES teacher education

Code	No.	Sex	Birth	Chi	PS	Formal Education
ASP	19	f	n/a	1	no	n/a
CAN	19	f	n/a	5	no	n/a
AGK	20	f	1984	1	yes	Catechist school
CCK	21	f	1988	0	no	PS teacher education

VT = 'vocational training', ES = 'elementary school', PS = 'primary school'.

All of the interviewees speak Tok Pisin fluently, but Qaqet is their first language. The education levels are quite diverse. Fifteen of the participants have finished Grade 6 of the Raunsepna primary school, four Grade 8. Four visited the secondary school outside of Raunsepna and finished Grade 10, while one woman left school after Grade 3. ABD and ACM are elementary teachers, CCK a primary teacher, and all teachers received their training outside of Raunsepna. Five participants received vocational training, three of whom are women. AGK and CCM have been trained as catechists. Thus, 14 out of 35 participants spent longer periods of their lives outside the village and its surroundings, and received extended formal education, which is not representative of Raunsepna. However, it is hardly surprising that those people most interested in participating in research are otherwise most curious about the world outside their village. During the interviews, in addition to agreeing or disagreeing with the statements, most participants supplemented their answers with statements in their own words and gave examples. These participant citations, which are exemplary of attitudes in Raunsepna, were transcribed and translated into English. They will be presented and analysed in the following text. This approach is dialogical, following a tradition framed by Duranti (2008: 87) among others:

> Rather than replacing native [sic!] discourse with the observer's monologic narrative (whether in the first or third person), as typical of analogical anthropology, dialogical anthropology promotes native talk to the position of prominence so as to give readers more direct access to how members represent their own actions as well as how they deal with fieldworkers and comply with their demands.

For each topic discussed, previous findings from the literature on Baining will first be presented, if available. Then the findings from the current study will be summarised and illustrated by citations from the interviews. Additionally, the number of participants who agreed or disagreed with the relevant statement from the interview guidelines will be reported.

This information will be given in brackets: (Question No.: number of interviews in which participants agreed with statement X/all participants who have been asked that question). The full results for all statements can be found in the Appendix.[5]

The next section starts with the description of Qaqet children's chore curriculum, which is framed by the community's lifestyle as subsistence farmers. Additionally, findings from participant observation will be employed if they deviate from the statements obtained during the interviews or add more information. If the data from both sources agree on a topic, no further comments will be made.

2.2.2 The chore curriculum: Living from the garden

As subsistence farmers (see Figures 2.1–2.3) mostly depending on the harvest of their gardens, the community members in Raunsepna highly value work in the garden. Villagers with large gardens who provide generously for their families and their guests are highly respected (Dickhardt 2009: 151). Children's chore curriculum, too, is framed by the task of becoming a successful subsistence farmer.

Figure 2.1: AMS on her way to the garden.
Source: Photograph by the author.

---

5   Note that not all the questions have been asked in all of the interviews as some people dropped out early.

Figure 2.2: AMS's children happy to see her coming to the garden.
Source: Photograph by the author.

Figure 2.3: AMS with her children on her way through the garden.
Source: Photograph by the author.

In the interviews, all of the participants (8: 20/20) agreed that children have to learn how to work in the garden. A quote from BCP illustrates this, see (1). Similar evidence on educational ideologies has been reported for Trobriand islanders by Senft and Senft (2018), among whom garden work figures as one of the leading rules in order to live a good life. For people depending entirely on their gardens for survival, this is hardly surprising.

(1) *Pasin bilong mipela, wok gaden em bikpela samting so mipela i laikim ol pikinini bai ol i mas bihainim mipela.*
'It is our custom that garden work is important, so we want our children to follow our example.' (BCP, Int_BCP_ARN)

In Raunsepna, children as young as three or four are able to fulfill household duties, as CCK in example (2) below describes it. This is normal in societies where the adults are typically engaged in activities that allow for the presence of children (Jensen & Gaskins 2015; Keller 2012; Lancy 2008).

(2) *So ol i lainim ol pikinini bilong ol olsem hia long kollektim paiawut, pulimap wara, halpim long wok gaden, em dispela.*
'So they teach their children to collect firewood, fetch water, help with the garden work, these kinds of things.' (CCK, Int_CCK)

Children as young as four years of age may be perfectly able to fulfill a range of duties and do so without anyone telling them, as two mothers reported (Int_AMT, Int_ABD_ACP). Those duties include lighting fires, finding leafy greens or staple foods in gardens close to the house, fetching water or firewood, or even cooking small meals (see Figure 2.4), sweeping the house, looking after animals or younger siblings (for short spans of time; see Figure 2.5), helping with washing the dishes, and helping with garden works like weeding (see Figure 2.6) and chasing parrots out of the peanut gardens.

Figure 2.4: ZCR carrying the food through the garden.
Source: Photograph by the author.

Figure 2.5: XSD carrying her baby brother ZLK.
Source: Photograph by the author.

Figure 2.6: YMN with a knife in the garden.
Source: Photograph by the author.

Already at a very early age, children are integrated into productive everyday life, and learn to act responsibly for others. Most interviewees confirmed that fetching water and wood would be the first tasks of children (7: 18/20). Two interviewees disagreed and explicated: before children learned to fetch water, they remarked, children would learn to go and fetch things inside the house. Gradually, then, the radius in which those children are expected to fetch things for others scales up. Everyone (11: 18/18) agreed that small children (who have just learned to walk independently) will be sent to accompany their older siblings, and learn by imitating what they do. The care of younger siblings constitutes a large part of children's responsibilities (13: 19/0) (see (3)).

(3) *Taim ol mama i lusim ol i go long gaden bai ol i lusim ol pikinini long han bilong ol bikpela bilong ol hia.*
'When the mothers leave the children to go to the garden, they leave them with their older siblings.' (AGK, Int_AGK)

Even four-year-old children may be left alone to watch over their baby siblings, but as all interviewees agreed, only for short periods of time. Children of around six may be left alone with younger siblings for entire days while the adults work in the garden. Hellwig (2020) reports a high degree of mobility for children in Raunsepna. They are quite unrestricted in that they frequently roam the village among themselves. This, too, is typical of rural subsistence-based cultures, as opposed to the typical lives of many children in post-industrial, urban societies that frequently take place in mother-infant-dyads first and under the supervision of other adults later, following fixed timetables (Lancy 2012b; Lieven 1994). All interviewees (17: 16/16) agreed that from around six or seven years of age, boys and girls in Raunsepna begin to have slightly different duties.

While boys learn how to build a fence, cut trees and make a new garden, girls mainly learn to weed in the garden and fulfill tasks related to the household (see (4)).

(4) *Especially long mipela, ol pikinini meri, mipela mas lainim ol long wit. Bikos ol man, em i wok bilong ol long katim bus, katim diwai i go daun.*
'Especially for us, the girls, we have to teach them how to weed. Because the men, their work is to clear the bush, cut the trees.' (ABD, INT_ABD_ACP)

Still, this division is not entirely fixed, household duties may be shared especially among married people, as two women remarked (see (5)).

(5) *Long family yet, tupela wantaim bai mekim ol dispela wok, hia. Taim olsem mama em i go long gaden na papa em i stap, em i ken kuk. Em i ken swip.*
'Inside the family, both share these jobs. If for example the mother goes to the garden and the father stays, he can cook. He can sweep.' (CCK, INT_CCK)

If children are asked to fulfill specific tasks, people usually expect that they will do so. Obedience is described as an important moral value for the Qaqet community by Dickhardt (2009). However, if children express unwillingness, usually, after some prompts, they are not forced into work. A certain degree of individual autonomy is highly accepted in the community: mood changes in a person are respected, even in children. When asked what to do if a child really does not want to carry out a specific task, participants frequently comment *larim em!* 'leave him/her!' In interaction with children, however, I frequently observed how parents tried to persuade children by offering rewards or threatening punishments. In Raunsepna, children are perceived as eager to work (see (6)). All interviewees reported situations like the ones cited below, where children ask to participate in working activities. If children want to imitate adults working, they are usually supported (6: 20/20; see (6)).

(6) *Olsem liklik BK bilong mi. Mi sikirap, bai karai. Bai mi givim em singapu bai sikirapim.*
'Just like my small BK. I scrape taro, she cries. So I give her the Singapore taro to scrape.' (ABD, Int_ABD_ACP)

However, two interviewees mentioned that tools would not be handed over in situations where the parents need the tool the child is asking for. Sharp bush knives are not given to very small children. In those cases, one interviewee commented, it would be useful to provide safer tools like blunt knives to satisfy the children. Children are allowed to handle a variety of objects that might be perceived as dangerous by Western parents, and are hence allowed a great deal of autonomy in the sense of Keller (2012). Still, parents monitor their children attentively so that the risk stays within certain limits, and they can intervene, if necessary. As (6) shows, children are perceived as being able to initiate learning in Raunsepna (see Section 2.1). People described the normal style of learning as observational (2: 20/20), as in (7):

(7) *Papa i no inap tokim em olsem: Yu mekim dispela, yu mekim dispela, nogat. Ol i mekim – em tu em i lainim long–wanem samting em i wok long lukim.*
'The father would not tell them like this: You make this, you make this, no. They do it – He will learn from – what he sees.' (CCK, Int_CCK)

Instead of explicit instruction, children in Raunsepna learn through guided participation, which is typical in non-WEIRD societies (Rogoff et al. 1993). Still, when children fail to imitate successfully, they will be corrected. This might be a case where they damage things in the garden (see (8)).

(8) *Taim em i stat wok yu mas lukluk long em: 'Em taro hia, nogut yu katim. Yu lukaut long ol samting mama i bin planim.'*
'When she starts to work you have to watch her: 'That's taro, don't cut it. Be careful with the things your mother has planted.' (AAS, Int_AAS)

The first attempts of children of around two to four to imitate their parents' or siblings' work are not perceived as really useful, but nevertheless instructive (see (9)).

(9) *Em kain pilai bilong ol. Ol i wok long lainim nau– long wokim alluska nau. Em bai stap bai wokim paia, bai putim siton, bai kisim ol liklik kumu gras, bai wok long wokim nau– Em i lainim nau.*
'It's like a kind of game for them. They are learning now–to work steamed greens now. He will stay and make a fire, put stones, then take the leafy greens, he's working it now–He learns it now.' (ABD, Int_ABD_ACP)

All the interviewees (21: 18/18) agreed that children's very first attempts to imitate others' work are a kind of 'play' but are at the same time instructive. The *pilai* 'play' here seems to be used to denote an activity that is opposed to work that makes a 'real' contribution.

2.2.3 Children's play

2.2.3.1 Attitudes to play

Play has significant beneficial effects for various aspects of language development (Levy 1984; Akinyi Ojuondo 2015). Just to highlight a few of these, play creates a variety of learning opportunities for various kinds of language use, and stimulates innovation and the use of new words and concepts (Bruner 1985). While children obviously learn to speak in all societies, how they do so depends on their everyday activities, which is why the current section explores the topic of child play among the Qaqet Baining.

Gaskins et al. (2007) describe three types of societies that differ with respect to the value they attribute to child play. In urban, middle class, Western societies, play is cultivated and caregivers are expected to spend time and effort to support it. In other societies, play is culturally accepted, and valued as an activity that keeps children out of the way. On the other extreme of the scale are societies that curtail play like the Yucatec Maya (Jensen & Gaskins 2015). In her ethnography of the Baining people, Fajans (1997: 92) states that child play is little valued and frequently suppressed by adult Bainings, who devalue it as animalistic behaviour, opposed to work, which is valued as an activity that transforms natural things into cultural ones. These claims are based on data from life cycle interviews where people report that their parents once got angry as they were playing. Additionally, Fajans refers to her own observation:

> There is very little child culture among the Baining. The Baining do not consider that children learn from play. Parents do not make toys for their children. They do not give them miniatures of adult objects such as spears, baskets, tools etc. They rarely play with their children in a verbal or active way. (Fajans 1997: 92)

She argues that 'the Baining attempt to prevent children from playing, on the grounds that to play is to behave as an animal (i.e., in an asocial or 'natural' way)' (Fajans 1997: 7). With reference to these claims, Lancy

(2015) cites the Baining as the only society where children do not play. If that were true, it would have significant consequences for contexts in which language acquisition takes place.

However, while there is much variation between different societies regarding the attitudes to child play and the forms it takes (Jensen & Gaskins 2015), even in societies where play is curtailed, 'children do spend time playing, their play takes varied forms, and it is clearly an enjoyable activity' (Gaskins et al. 2007: 197).

Among the Baining, Fajans observed only few activities she identified as 'play'. While she does not offer any definition of 'play', she compares the children's activities to those of animals:

> One explanation [for the adults' negative attitude towards child play] might be related to the fact that the games played by children are not very structured or organized. They do not involve social values like work or reciprocity. Most of the games are forms of running, chasing, splashing, and throwing things. Such activities are both noisy and disorderly. They seem more animalistic than human. I hypothesize that it is this aspect that parents object to. (Fajans 1997: 92)

Given the attitude to children's play evident from the quote above, it seems hardly surprising that Baining children had little motivation to play in the researcher's presence (see also Section 1.3.3).

Gray (2019: 85f), following Vygotsky (1978), identifies as main criteria for playful activity (in young children) enjoyment, flexibility, and pretense/nonliterality out of the five criteria presented originally by Krasnor and Pepler (1980). For the description of children's play activities in Raunsepna, I will adapt this definition. While I cannot be sure that this definition is shared by the interview participants, as I did not discuss their concept of play with them, the examples they provided mostly fit the above criteria.

In the interviews, adults stressed several important functions of child play: all participants (20: 20/20) confirmed that children do need play as recreational activity. Moreover, most participants (22: 17/20) regarded play as an educational medium as example (10) illustrates.

(10)   *Pilai bai lainim ol planti samting.*
       'Play will teach them many things.' (ACM, Int_ACM_AML)

While 15 interviewees agreed that without play (as an educational or recreational activity) children would not be able to learn to work, in three interviews, people agreed that play was not necessary to learn to work. Even more interviewees were skeptical about the statement 'All parents everywhere have to play with their children'. Only 11 agreed, five explicitly disagreed and commented that they do not know about other countries. In addition to the recreational and instructive functions, another aspect of children's play frequently referred to in the interviews is the bonding effect (see (11)). There was no question referring to this in the questionnaire, so only two speakers' self-initiated reports are presented here.

(11) *Olsem mipela long hia, mipela i sa hamamas long ol pikinini na pilai long ol, mipela i lainim ol tu olsem long ol liklik ol pilai ol dispela kain.*
'It's like this, we over here, we are happy about our children and play with them, we teach them also those small games and the like.'
(AMM, Int_AMM_AVD)

DCK in example (12) also comments that children are explicitly taught little games, some of which have already been taught by previous generations before to present-day adults.

(12) *Olsem mipela i bin gro ap na ol lapun mama bilong mipela ol i tok 'bipo, taim bilong mipela, mipela sa pilai olsem.'*
'Just like when we were growing up and our old mothers said to us: "In our times, we played like this".' (DCK, Int_ASQ_DCK)

Having addressed the attitudes towards the value and functions of play, I will now turn to the forms of play and who participates in play with reference to pictures from Raunsepna and sometimes Kamanakam, wherever possible. I will especially address the issue of adults' participation in these games. The types and definitions follow those proposed by Smith (2008).

2.2.3.2 Types of play in Raunsepna

I witnessed various occasions where adults played **social contingency play** with infants and toddlers, trying to make them smile about the adults' actions or reactions. Especially women frequently try to distract crying babies with such activities. Alternatively, they may pass them all kinds of everyday items to enable them to indulge in **sensorimotor play**, experiencing the sensory properties of objects.

I often observed **pretend play**: children imitate adult activities such as garden work, cooking, selling market produce, or imitating the traditional dances. These are the forms of play that are referred to by adults when they describe how play may teach them to fulfill their duties. However, Qaqet adults may even say that a child plays when she actually does help harvesting peanuts but is not focused and therefore not efficient. In the longitudinal corpus, we have several recordings of children engaging in **language games** such as the word repetition game described by Fajans (1997: 92). From these games, children may not only learn words for things, but even how to use possessive constructions or noun class suffixes (Hellwig & Jung 2020). As already noted by Fajans (1997: 92), children, usually in groups, frequently engage in **physical activity play**, running or climbing around or swimming in the stream (see Figure 2.7). Gosso et al. (2019) emphasises the value of these activities 'for the quality and viability of their childhood when they face the challenges and risks of their physical environment in their free and unsupervised daily play activities'. Some of these activities may involve objects found in the environment (see Figure 2.8a and 2.8b). Usually, the children play with them among themselves, but occasionally, adults may offer assistance (see Figure 2.8b).

Figure 2.7: Children playing in the stream.
Source: Photograph by Carmen Dawuda, with permission.

Both in groups and solitarily, children engage in **object play**. While there are few industrialised toy items, there are various toys made from bush material. The most frequent one is the *karki* 'car' (see Figure 2.9a), consisting of a long stick with a wheel of bamboo or wood attached to its end. It is frequently made by fathers for their children, but also by older siblings.

Other bush material toys are propeller-toys (see Figure 2.9b), stilts (see Figure 2.10a), or a ball made of the pith of a tree (see Figure 2.10b and Figure 2.10c). Additionally, parents may provide all kinds of everyday-items like rubber bands (Figure 2.11b) or grasshoppers (Figure 2.9c). Apart from the forms of play described above, there are also rule-governed games in Raunsepna.

With infants, adults may play rhythmic finger games (*aqerliska*, *aqalevupka*). The players grasp each other's hands (see Figure 2.11a), then they sing a short song. Each time it is finished, the player whose hand is at the bottom has to remove it and put it on the top again. String figure games (see Figure 2.11c) are played alone or with several players by manipulating strings in order to form multiple figures.

Older children, especially girls, frequently play a stone game: seven stones are distributed on the ground. The player throws one stone in the air and has to pick up one stone from the ground before catching the stone she threw into the air. This is repeated, though the player has to pick up first two, then three stones, and so on. Once she has picked up all stones from the ground, she throws them all up again, trying to catch as many of them as possible with the back of her hand. Many of these games and toys have also been observed by Senft and Senft (2018) among Trobriand children, such as string figure games, swings, palm leaf sleighs, stilts and even a similar 'pretend car' (see Figure 2.9a). Hoenigman (2020) describes string figure games among the Awiakay in Eastern Sepik Province (PNG).

Figure 2.8a: Two children playing with a part of a broken mower.
Source: Photograph by Carmen Dawuda, with permission.

Figure 2.8b: AMS helping her children to swing on liana.
Source: Photograph by the author.

Figure 2.9 Children engaging playfully with their environment.
Source: Photographs by the author.
Note:
(a) A toy karki, often built by parents or older siblings for small children.
(b) J with a self-made propeller-toy his mother taught him to build.
(c) XAT playing with a grasshopper whose legs have been torn out by his mother so it cannot run away.

Figure 2.10: Various items used as toys by Qaqet children.
Source: photographs by the author.
Note:
(a) Children walking on stilts their parents made for them.
(b) ZCL and ZTT carving a ball from the pith of a tree under supervision of their mother.
(c) The ball.

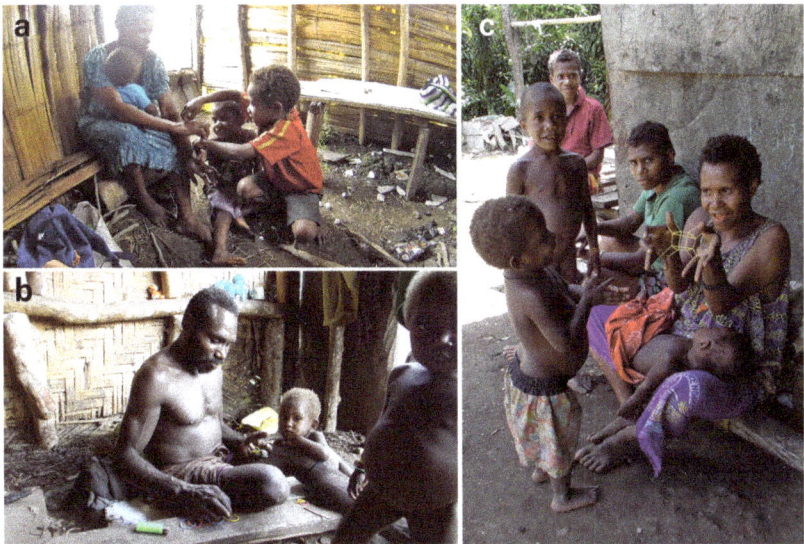

Figure 2.11: Parents in Raunsepna as they play with their children.
Source: Photographs by the author.
Note:
(a) ARN teaching her children a fingergame called aqerliska.
(b) DCK sorting ZEA's rubber bands for her to play with.
(c) ARN teaching her children a string game.

In this section I have presented evidence that Qaqet children engage in various forms of play, including rule-governed play. Furthermore, I have shown that adults do not suppress play, but may even value it for its instructive, recreational or bonding effects and offer support or guidance. The next section will deal with restrictions on play.

2.2.3.3 Play and respect

While child play in Raunsepna today is ubiquitous, its reception still depends on the context of the situation. It also happens that groups of children are told to be quiet or leave the place where they are currently playing so as to not disturb adults.

All of the interviewees (25: 19/19) agreed with the statement that children can be sent away and that it is a matter of respect not to disturb adults. This is exemplified in (13):

(13) a. ABK: *Olsem sapos mitupela i gat wanpela poroman i kam mipela i laik toktok long sampela samting em i ...*
'So, if the two of us have a friend who visits and we want to talk about something that is ...'
b. ARB: *Tupela i wok long sindaun insait na tupela i wok long pilai, bai mitupela i rausim tupela insait long haus, bai tupela i go pilai arasait.*
'The two sit inside and play, so we will tell them to leave the house and play outside.'
c. ADK: *Em – em – wanpela part bilong rispek, aah? Sapos tupela i laik stap, bai tupela i mas sidaun isi, aah?*
'That is– that is– a matter of respect, yeah? If they want to stay, they have to sit down quietly, yeah?' (Int_ARB_ADK)

In (13) ARB and ADK express their expectation that children have to respect adults' affairs. Below, I address respect as a value every interviewee confirmed as an important driving principle of Baining child education. The study by Dickhardt (2009) about morality among the Qaqet Baining is based on fieldwork conducted mostly in the village of Raunsepna. He describes several key dimensions of morality, comprising work, generosity and sharing, respect, allegiance, and shame as highly valued in the community. While all of these values have been referred to in the interviews, respect and shame figured especially prominently: respect towards other people and the resulting shame if one has behaved in a disrespectful manner are guiding principles of social interaction (Dickhardt 2009: 155). This has been especially emphasised by all interviewees with respect to what a child has to acquire in order to become a successful member of the Qaqet Baining society.

Respect entails caring for others, especially guests, not humiliating others, valuing their property and avoiding direct conflict (Dickhardt 2009). During the primary interviews, people frequently mentioned shame as a distinguishing trait of the Baining people. The same is reported by Dickhardt (2009: 160) to whom Raunsepna was introduced as *peles bilong sem* 'place of'. Children are taught with care to share, be generous and behave properly. Shame can also be caused by misbehaviour of adults' own children (see 14).

(14) *Em bai bringim sem i go long papa na mama bikos tupela i no wok long lainim pikinini.*
'That will bring shame to the father and the mother because they are not teaching the child.' (ABD, Int_ABD_ACP)

Reasons to be ashamed of the behaviour of one's children include disrespectful behaviour towards elders, laziness or stealing food. Stealing is highly stigmatised, whereas sharing, conversely, is highly valued (Dickhardt 2009: 153).

The generous provision, especially of food, for others is also a central principle of social life in Raunsepna (Dickhardt 2009: 153–55). Small children have to learn early to break their food and share it with their fellows, as all interviewees (29: 18/18) confirm. The youngest child, many interviewees (30: 14/18) agreed, takes on a special position. Babies usually get what they want and older siblings are expected to give up food in favour of the youngest. Altogether, as the current section has shown, generous and respectful behaviour towards other people, mixed with a belief in children's autonomous will to learn, frame child education in Raunsepna.

Similar observations hold also for child language acquisition.

2.2.4 Language attitudes and attitudes to child language acquisition

Marley (2013) investigated language choice between Tok Pisin and Qaqet, conducting her fieldwork entirely in the village of Raunsepna. She reports that language use is determined mainly by a person's perceived insider or outsider status: the former prompting Qaqet use, the latter Tok Pisin use. Children, according to Marley's data, are perceived as pure Qaqet speakers and mostly prompt the use of Qaqet (Marley 2013: 122–32). The Qaqet see themselves as responsible for the language acquisition of their children and say that they explicitly correct non-target-like forms (Marley 2013: 132).

For the Uramot Baining (or Ura),[6] Stanton (2007) reports slightly different insights from interviews about language attitudes: mothers especially take responsibility for the language of children, contrary to the perception among the Qaqet in Raunsepna that this is the task of both parents. Parents feel ashamed when their children produce non-target-like forms but still do not dare to correct these. Non-target-like Ura is conceived of as 'baby talk' and highly stigmatised. Ura fathers, unlike

---

6   Uramot is another language of the six members from the Baining family. The Ura live south of the Qaqet.

Qaqet fathers in Raunsepna, talk only Tok Pisin to their children instead of Ura. Nevertheless, the opinion prevails that children 'must learn their language well' (Stanton 2007) and mixed marriage is perceived as the main reason for language shift.

In the interview sessions, all people from Raunsepna (45/46: 20/20) agreed that children learn language because people talk to them (see (15)).

(15) *I qerl nani nyitaqen branini de nani ini ngatat*
'It's like this, you talk to the little ones and they learn it.' (ARL, INT_ARL_AMS)

One mother (see (16)) explicitly emphasised that talking even to newborn babies is important, despite all doubts that they are able to understand:

(16) *Baby, yu karim em stret na yu mas toktok long em. Yu noken ting olsem im i no inap harim.*
'When your baby is born then you have to start to talk to her/him. You must not think she/he does not understand.' (BLN, INT_APA_BLN)

An example everyone provided when I asked about how to teach a child language is what I will call a 'fetching routine'. Interactional routines (Bruner 1985; de León Pasquel 2011) are sequentially organised, repeated communicative acts that offer a niche for the child to participate in a given communicative exchange (de León Pasquel 2011: 96). They express 'values embedded in the culture and social structure' (Peters & Boggs 1986: 94). Through repetition of the interaction, the children can gradually draw the connections between the phrases and the actions or things they denote. Finally, the children themselves can become agents in the situation.

In example (17) a mother asks her son (12 months) to fetch the water bottle for her, which is lying next to him.

(17) *G.! Nyit tama kainaqi ip ngusup!*
'G.! Go and fetch the water for me to drink!' (AMS, INT_ARL_AMS)

Even small babies are sometimes given items like a betel nut and are told to give it to someone else, who then thanks the baby. In the opinion of the interviewees, the fetching routine is how children are taught words. Small children are regularly sent to fetch different kinds of objects, at first inside and around the house where people can point to the desired object. The pointing was described by everyone (56: 21/21) as necessary to help the child identify the intended referent. I witnessed that elder children are regularly sent around for errands, especially to fetch all kinds of items. Messenger services are a typical task for children. With the fetching routine, young children are socialised early into their roles within their society, while simultaneously acquiring the words for things (and possibly names of places and people).

A similar routine figured in the comparative data for CDS and ADS. I will refer to this as the 'where routine' (see (18) with XAT, 34 months, and his father).

(18) a. XAT: *hoskiqua?*
'Where is the horse?'
b. ARL: *lira nyitluqi iqiatit*
'You have seen it walking just before.'
c. XAT: *hoskiqua?*
'Where is the horse?'
d. XAT: *kiatit kua?*
'Where does it go?'
e. ARL: *lamuk manem*
'There on the picture.'
f. XAT: *manemgua?*
'Where is the picture?'
g. ARL: *lamuk!*
'There!' (PearARLP 17-24)

XAT uses the where routine in a recursive style. He does not only ask for the location of the horse, like in (18a), but every time ARL answers his question he repeats the question for the new object of reference proposed by his father. Hellwig (2020) reports that in experimental settings with children and adults in Raunsepna the 'where' questions seemed most natural for them. During visits to the family's house, I witnessed the routine frequently initiated by XAT's mother, AMS, who enjoyed pursuing it into a near-infinite regress like the one also demonstrated by XAT. Hence not only children, but also adults towards children, make use of the routine as several other examples in the comparative corpus confirm. From my own experience in the everyday life of Raunsepna, I am aware of the salience of the topic of locations in everyday culture. The typical questions as one meets someone else around the village are 'Where are you going?', 'Where are you coming from?' and 'Where is… (a person, a thing)?'. The importance of location and direction has also been noted in other communities that maintain a close connection to their land. For example, among Kwara'ae people on Malaita in the Solomon Islands, the 'where' question is used to distract crying children and calm them down (Watson-Gegeo & Gegeo 1986). I witnessed this also in Raunsepna; even if there was nothing to be detected, the children would still be distracted by trying to spot something. A similar situation is described by Bavin (2004) for Warlpiri speakers in Australia. She found that even four- to five-year-old children use locatives frequently, which is explained by the close connection to the land and the resulting salience of locations in daily interactions.

With the where routine, children have the chance to learn labels for things around them, as well as words describing locations. Moreover, while learning the linguistic means for talking about locations, they are socialised into a cultural context that attaches high importance to orientation. All instances I witnessed took place between children and their parents, reflecting the attitude expressed by the participants in the interviews. All interviewees (42: 20/20) confirmed that parents are responsible for their children's proper language acquisition, confirming Marley's results from 2011. All interviewees (62: 20/20) agreed that children's non-target-like forms have to be corrected and most (62: 19/20) agreed that you should do so even for other people's children. Children using incorrect language can bring shame upon their parents, who are blamed for not having taught them properly.

While most interviewees confirmed that everyone would talk to babies (49: 19/20), two interviewees said that it was usually mothers who talk to babies. One female interviewee even expressed the belief that fathers must not carry small babies, as their hands are too big, so they had few opportunities to talk to them. In fact, as long as children are breastfed, they are primarily carried by their mothers (Fajans 1997). In example (19), a speaker expresses the view that it is mostly the joy about the baby that makes particularly mothers talk to their babies, a view that all interviewees shared (47: 18/18).

(19) *Ol mama i gutpela long dispela. Taim pikinini ol i wok long kakarim na maski em i no save, tasol mama bai yu lukim em i wok long kakarim em i hamamas long em na em i wok long toktok long em.*
'The mothers are good at this. When the child, they are carrying him/her around and although he/she does not know, but the mother you see her carrying him/her around, she is so happy about him/her and is talking to him/her.' (DCM, INT_AMI_DCM)

All of the interviewees (58: 20/20) agreed that mothers sometimes modify their speech when they are addressing their small children. Only in 13 interviews people did agree that fathers also do so. A frequently cited example was the pronunciation of *nyisup!* 'you drink', which is rendered as *tup!* 'drink' in baby talk. With regard to the reasons for these adaptations, the interviewees commented that this change was due to an imitation of the child's own language (see (20)).

(20) *Tasol ol i sa bihainim pikinini. Taim pikinini em i lainim toktok em bai wok long tromoi ol dispela ol toktok 'tup'.*
'They are just imitating the child. When the child learns to talk he will use these kinds of words like *tup*.' (AGK, INT_AGK)

While some interviewees commented that this kind of speech adaptation might be helpful for the child (see (21)), most interviewees were more suspicious about this kind of change in speech (see (22)).[7]

(21) *Ol i bihainim stael blong pikinini bilong lainim ol.*
'They follow the style of the child in order to teach them.' (AMT, INT_AMT)

(22) *Ol mama gen ol i save – paulim dispela toktok gen – Olsem taim yu lainim pikinini bilong yu long tokples long save long toktok yu lainim em gut. Olsem yu noken sotim ken olsem tup, tup – nyisup, nyisup!*
'The mothers again they – they make this talk wrong again – Like this, when you teach your child to talk the vernacular you should teach him/her well. Like this, you should not shorten again like *tup, tup – nyisup, nyisup!*' (AGK, INT_AGK)

The doubts are primarily expressed towards those features that seem to be imitating the children's limited capacity, which expresses the worry that children might not learn the language properly. However, a short utterance length (an example explicitly mentioned by several interviewees) and a slow speech rate (61: 20/20) were acknowledged by all interviewees as helpful for comprehension.

Adults are thus considered primarily responsible for proper language acquisition in their children, and they consider them communicative partners. Still, I observed that it is often the older child who is the primary addressee of utterances. As young children spend a large portion of the day

---

7   I did not include this question in the interview guidelines, therefore no numbers are provided.

in the company of older siblings, they acquire a central role as interlocutors. Once children are old enough to join their siblings in play, it is mainly the siblings, all the interviewees (53: 18/18) agreed, who teach each other the language. This opinion confirms research reporting a high amount of sibling childcare in non-WEIRD societies (see Section 2.1). Through contact with other children, many children may also acquire their first knowledge of Tok Pisin (Marley 2013). It is seen as positive by everyone (44: 17/17) when children learn Tok Pisin. The language is appreciated as a means to communicate with outsiders, confirming the results of Marley (2013). In example (23), one speaker expresses the view that it causes shame when an outsider approaches her and she cannot understand him or her.

(23) *Nogut wanpela i kam na toktok long yu na yu sidaun olsem.*
'Otherwise it might happen that someone comes and talks to you and you just sit there like that.' (BRS, INT_BRS_DRN)

Still, all the interviewees (41: 18/18) agreed that children have to acquire Qaqet first. The importance of the Qaqet language is mainly associated with its deep connection to the culture (see (24)).

(24) *Tokples bilong yu yet i sa strongim kastem, pasin sa stap insait long em.*
'Your vernacular strengthens your culture, the good behaviour lies within it.' (AAS, INT_AAS)

People perceive the connection between language and culture to be very strong, which was also described for the Mali Baining by Stebbins (2004) and by Stanton (2007) for the Ura Baining. This may also provoke a certain indignation when people are asked about those parts of Baining land where language shift has already gone further into the direction of Tok Pisin (see (25)).

(25) *Mipela i laik strongim dispela dignity na identity bilong mipela, ol Baining. Bikos kastem em bikpela samting. Sapos mipela i strongim, em bai stap tasol. Bikos mipela i lukim nau long nambis, kastem em i lus pinis. Nau i ol i save singautim mipela long hia long taim bilong Firedance.*
'We want to strengthen our, the Bainings', identity and dignity. Because our traditions are important. If we strengthen them, they will stay. Because we see it now at the coast, the traditions are already lost. Now they call us for the times of Firedance.'[8] (ACM, INT_ACM_AML)

---

8   The Baining firedance is famous in all of Papua New Guinea. Dancers incorporating spirits with spectacular masks dance at night and step into the fire. In order to know the appropriate lyrics for the songs, good Qaqet knowledge is indispensable.

The reason for the language shift is mainly seen to be mixed marriages, confirming earlier research about Baining people (see Section 2.1). Participants perceive a strong connection between the arrival of outsiders from different regions of Papua New Guinea, intermarriage and the loss of their vernacular. In those regions, children would not be taught properly (see (26)).

(26) *kuasiqiretaqasu aruisa!*
'They do not teach their children properly!' (AMS, INT_ARL_AMS)

Still, for Raunsepna, the interviewees perceived the strength of the vernacular to be more stable than at the coast, in line with the results from Marley: there are few outsiders who trigger the use of Tok Pisin, and Qaqet is spoken in most domains of life, resulting in a healthy language situation (Marley 2013: 150). All of the interviewees (39: 20/20) expressed a strong interest in keeping their vernacular alive. Code-mixing is regarded with suspicion (see (27)).

(27) *Noken abusim toktok, noken mixim toktok!*
'You must not mix it, you must not mix the language!' (AGK, INT_AGK)

While this opinion is expressed frequently and firmly, I still witnessed numerous instances of code-mixing. The strong attitudes against this language practice must not be seen as reflecting everyday language choices but rather as an expression of worry about the growing dominance of Tok Pisin in various domains of everyday life, even though Qaqet is still strong in Raunsepna. Child language is often the main trajectory of language shift, as Kulick (1992) demonstrates in his description of the language shift of Taiap towards Tok Pisin. A language may have large numbers of speakers, but as soon as children do not learn it anymore, it is severely endangered. In this section, I have presented data on the attitudes prevailing in Raunsepna concerning various areas of life that are relevant for the language socialisation of young children. In a next step, the data on attitudes presented in the current section will be supplemented by a preliminary study on the amount of input three young children from Raunsepna receive.

2.3 The amount of input

Societies differ with regard to the amount and source of children's language input, as explained in the literature review in Section 1.2. Various researchers have reported that in non-WEIRD settings, young children receive less input overall and spend more time under the supervision of older siblings. Given that the adults in Raunsepna are busy with garden work during the day, similar patterns to this are to be expected.

In this section, the results of a pilot study are presented, which is intended: a) to provide a rough estimate of what children do and hear during a day in their life; and b) to test the methodology to allow for a large-scale study in the future.

This chapter reports on the quantitative and qualitative patterns found in audio-recordings of three children from Raunsepna. However, the reader should keep in mind that these patterns are probably not representative for Raunsepna as a whole due to methodological obstacles described in Section 2.3.1. Instead, this study is meant to provide a first impression of the amount of children's linguistic input in locally typical contexts and participant constellations.

2.3.1 Methods and data

I identified four families who had children within the desired age range (around 24–48 months). Another important consideration was that they were familiar enough with me and the linguistic work so as to be willing to try out a new method of data collection. The mean age of the children is 33 months. Two of the children, YDS (37 months) and ZDL (29 months), are focal children in the longitudinal study (see Section 1.4). The other children were XAT (35 months) and ZEA (32 months).

To record their daily interactions, the children carried a little woven bag. An audio-recorder (Zoom H2) was placed inside and the bag was closed with cable ties to prevent the children from playing with the audio-recorder. From the second recording session onward, the parents prepared the setup on their own. They were advised to monitor the children (or have siblings do so), to ensure they were carrying the bag, but otherwise to continue their usual, everyday work.

The children needed a certain amount of time to get used to the bag. Two of them (ZDL and YDS) did not adapt easily, and during the first sessions the bag was handed over quite quickly to their older siblings. Those data were excluded from the analysis. For YDS, who fell asleep during one other recording, there were no data left for which we could be sure that she was awake, hence her data are not part of the following analysis. First impressions from the few recordings of her data nevertheless confirm the high amount of individual variation. Due to the exclusion of YDS's data, the mean age of the children dropped to 32 months.

For the first recordings, I did not communicate clearly enough that the audio-recorder would not only record the children's talk but also everyone else talking around the child. For the focal families experienced with recordings that was obvious, but one family was surprised to hear their own voices on the recordings afterwards. As a result, I offered to exclude the data of these participants from the study and delete it. Thus, three sessions (i.e. three days of recording) for the participant ZEA were excluded. Altogether, 38 hours of recording had to be excluded from the analysis. The total amount of data used for the following counts is displayed in Table 2.3.

With the help of student assistants, the data were segmented in ELAN (equated with utterances, see Section 3.2.4 for details) and assigned to a speaker. Back in the field in 2017, I verified with the relevant families that the speakers were assigned correctly. Additionally, the speakers described the activities that the children pursued during the recording days. The data are not differentiated into overheard speech (henceforth OHS) and child-directed speech.

Table 2.3: Recorded hours per child.

Child	Hours
ZDL	1
ZEA	3
XAT	10
Total	14

2.3.2 Results and discussion

Table 2.4 shows the mean number of utterances the children heard per hour, combining directed and overheard speech. Utterances are equated with intonation units (see Section 4.2 for a discussion). The results are compared with those found for Yucatec Mayan children and children from Chicago in a study by Shneidman and Goldin-Meadow (2012) who analysed one hour of video-recording for each child. The Qaqet children and the Yucatec children hear much less speech than the children from Chicago. Shneidman and Goldin-Meadow (2012) remark, however, that their results probably underestimate the Mayan children's input as participants had difficulties in adapting to the recording situation, and produced fewer utterances than when not recorded.

Table 2.4: Utterances per hour, containing overheard speech (OHS) and CDS; Qaqet in comparison with results from Shneidman and Goldin-Meadow (2012).

Community, Age (months)	Utt./hr
Qaqet, 32	527
Yuc. Maya, 24	490
Yuc. Maya, 33	351
Chicago, 23	1,127
Chicago, 30	1,601

Table 2.5: Input (in utterances per hour) for the different child participants.

Speaker	ZDL	ZEA	XAT
Mother	184	139	104
Father	276	1	143
Siblings	306	90	30
Other children	38	5	1
Other adults	207	30	28
Total Utt./hr	1,011	265	306

Still, a closer look at the data from the current study reveals that the number of utterances heard by individual children differs vastly. Table 2.5 displays the rate at which the children heard utterances from different speaker groups. While ZDL heard 1,011 utterances per hour, resembling the children from Chicago, XAT (35 months) with 306 utterances per hour, and ZEA (32 months) with 265 utterances per hour, had values even below those of the Mayan children.

However, preliminary data from the sub-corpus of the longitudinal data comprising 22:40:29 hours of recordings containing the two children YDS (aged 23–29 months) and YRA (aged 38–44 months) indicate that the rates in the current study are not representative, either. In Table 2.6 it can be seen that ZDL heard fewer utterances per hour than in the current data, but both children received more input than ZEA and XAT in the current data.[9]

Concerning the speaker groups from which the children receive the most input, compared to the Mayan data from Shneidman and Goldin-Meadow (2012), the input of the Qaqet children in this study is exactly reversed. While the Mayan children received 31 per cent of their total input from adults and 69 per cent from children, the Qaqet children in the current data received 31 per cent from children and 69 per cent from adults.

Again, preliminary results from the longitudinal sub-corpus show a different pattern: the children mostly spend the day with their mother in the garden. By far the largest part of their input (68 per cent) is produced by other children.

Table 2.6: Preliminary data extraction from the longitudinal corpus (Hellwig et al. 2014–19).

	ZDL	YDS
Age range	2;01.05–2;02.11	2;01.03–2;02.03
Amount of recording	3:10:00 hours	3:30:41 hours
Utt./hr (input)	900.1	704.9
Utt./hr (child)	658.4	270.6

The results from the current study can be explained by independently investigating the data from each child, with reference to the activities pursued during the recording sessions. Figure 2.12 shows the percentage of speech each child in the current study heard from the different speaker groups.

---

9   A future examination of the longitudinal corpus offers the possibility to carefully match comparable situations, and would therefore produce more representative results. The data presented here nevertheless allow for some hypotheses.

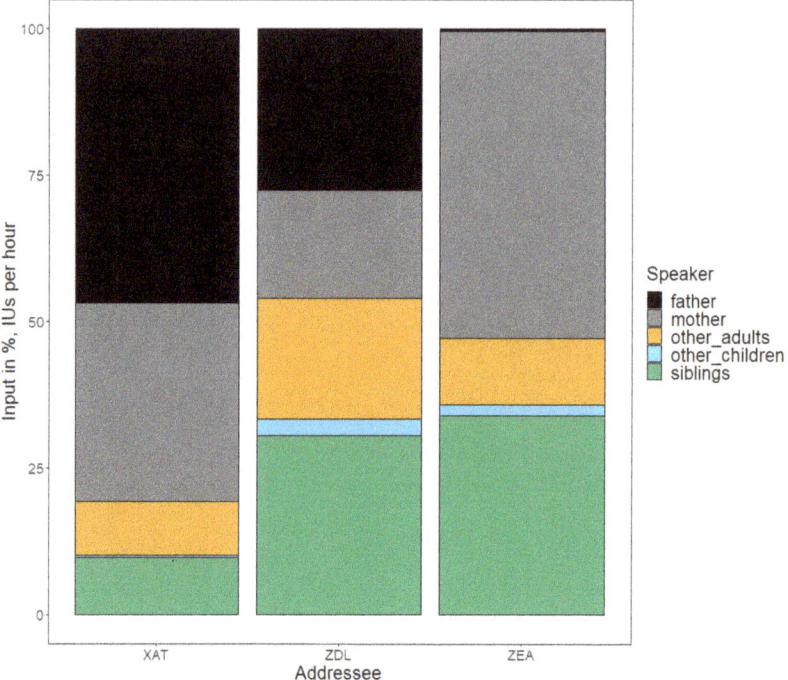

Figure 2.12: Input by speaker group and child, IUs per hour.

There are large differences among the children. In order to make sense of this variation, it is helpful to examine closely each child's individual situation. The youngest speaker, ZDL, is at home with his family. Both parents and all his siblings are present, as well as some visiting adults with their children. The adults are busy talking to each other. This results in a large amount of talk from unrelated adults (21 per cent) and both parents (18 per cent from the mother and 27 per cent from the father). The children play among themselves, 30 per cent of what ZDL hears comes from siblings, but only 4 per cent from the other children. ZDL himself produces 181 utterances per hour; accordingly, it is reasonable to expect that some of the others' talk is also directed towards him. For this family, as I witnessed during numerous visits at their house, the situation is very typical. There are often visitors around and large group communication contexts are the norm. The same is also confirmed by first impressions from the longitudinal data.

ZEA is mostly alone at home with her mother and her twin sister, so 53 per cent of all utterances she hears stem from her mother and 34 per cent from siblings. Some older siblings and a cousin living nearby play close to the house, accounting for the 2 per cent of input from other children. The father is working in the garden close to the house, and does not talk at all. Most of the communication takes place between the mother and the two small girls. Just as another woman passes by, the mother talks to her, resulting in 11 per cent of input from other adults.

XAT is the only child for whom recordings from two different days could be used. During the first day, XAT is sitting with the parents, two siblings, an aunt and a cousin around the cooking fire, where the women are busy preparing the meal and feeding the children. Thirty-four per cent of the utterances XAT hears over the two days stem from the mother and 10 per cent from other adults. During the second recording session, the initial setting is much the same, but afterwards, XAT accompanies his father to the garden. From there on, for four hours, it is only the two of them who communicate with each other, resulting in 47 per cent input from the father. XAT is a talkative child, and involves his father in extensive conversation.

This study was designed to gain a preliminary impression of the input that children receive. The number of utterances the children hear per hour is largely comparable to what has been reported for Yucatec Mayan children (Shneidman & Goldin-Meadow 2012), while it is much less than what the children from Western, urban contexts received in the same study. The difference between the individual children who participated in the current study is large, not only in the amount of input but also with regard to the children's interlocutors. The individual results can be explained with reference to the context and the resulting participant structure. Moreover, parents' daily duties, the talkativeness of the children themselves, and of their interlocutors, shapes what a child hears and how much she or he interacts with others.

The study nevertheless offers first insights into the types of communicative situations of children in Raunsepna. Families staying at their village house prefer to receive many visitors, resulting in a large amount of (probably overheard) speech from adults and much input from different children. If one adult is alone with a child, the chance is high that the child will hear a lot of directed input from that adult. This may happen, for example, when a father is in the garden with his son, as was the case for XAT in the current study. Equally, though, the father might be too busy with his work or simply might not be a talkative person. It is not the case, therefore, that children do not receive input from adults. Rather, the amount of input provided depends entirely on the context. The families of XAT and YDS often live in their gardens for extended periods of time, which usually results in little input from non-family members. In contrast, the families of ZDL and ZEA usually stay in their village house and therefore non-family members are frequently present.

The true salience of the different situation types and other factors in the life of each family and the amount of overheard and directed input the children receive can be assessed with a systematic comparison of the children's environments. This would require a larger data set than the current preliminary study offers. Careful sampling with attention to different situations and participation frameworks and differentiation between directed and overheard speech are necessary conditions to obtain representative results. Additionally, data from children spending time among themselves would have to be included, otherwise the percentage of input children receive from siblings might be severely underestimated.

2.4 Summary: Factors contributing to the language environment of children in Raunsepna

The current chapter is intended to contextualise the staged data in following chapters. In order to gain a full picture of the linguistic environments of young children in Raunsepna, the amount of input children receive and the attitudes and ideologies of people towards diverse aspects of child language socialisation have been described.

While the amount of speech the children hear can be compared to results from previous research on children's input in non-Western societies, the two data sets employed show conflicting tendencies regarding the speaker groups the children receive their input from. In the data collected for the present work, parents are the children's main conversation partners, while in the longitudinal data, it is the siblings who talk most to and around the children. This can again be thought of as an effect of the small sample size. Despite these criticisms, the study allows for valuable insights into the various factors that influence children's language environments. Personality, socialising habits and the timetables of their interlocutors shape children's linguistic worlds. While this first study underlines the necessity of keeping individual variation in mind, the discussion of attitudes shows the influence of shared realities and agreements. The interviewees reported that they see children as eager to learn, which is why they have to be given the freedom to do so on their own, without explicit instruction. Yet, correction was seen as appropriate if children do something that does not conform to the norm. Their core curriculum, typical for non-WEIRD, subsistence-based societies (Keller 2012; Lancy 2008), consists mainly of duties that may be learned through guided participation. That way, children are given partial responsibility for their community's wellbeing from early on, while they are gradually socialised into their roles. There is not much organised play under the supervision of adults, but contrary to claims in previous research, there is no evidence for suppression of play. On the contrary, most interviewees emphasised the educational, emotional, and recreational benefits of playing. Describing various forms of child play, I have presented evidence of the richness of child culture and even of the active participation of adults in this world.

Regarding attitudes towards language, all interviewees emphasised the deep importance of the Qaqet language. Some commented that they consider language and culture to be deeply connected to such an extent that the loss of the language would also cause their culture to disappear. This is what interviewees perceived as happening in more accessible coastal villages where children do not acquire Qaqet anymore. The interviewees blamed the parents of these children, as they hold the primary responsibility for their offspring's language acquisition. It is considered as a prerequisite for children's language acquisition that parents talk to their children, who then imitate them. This is different from what Kulick (1992) describes for Gapun, where people do not consider themselves as having an influence on their children's language acquisition. In Raunsepna, even small babies are addressed as conversational partners, contrary to reports by Ochs (1988) for Samoans or Schieffelin (1990) for the Kaluli. Adults consider it important to correct children's linguistic errors and may feel shame about children's non-target-like utterances. This is similar to the situation described by Stanton (2007) for the Ura. Presumably, the difference is just that among the Ura interviewees, language shift was already further advanced than among the Qaqet. Ura caregivers do not trust their own language competence and therefore do not correct their children. While Qaqet adult caregivers, especially parents, are seen as holding the main responsibility for their children's language development, siblings also play a salient role as frequent caregivers, like in many other small, rural language communities (Lieven 1994). Adults explicitly emphasise the importance of child interlocutors for children's language development.

There are conflicting opinions among adults in Raunsepna with regard to the way in which people talk to children or should talk to them. People agree that mothers usually do adapt their speech to children, but not everyone thought that fathers do so. They provided examples of phonetic changes and a few words of a babytalk lexicon. Many were critical about the effects of what they perceive as 'incorrect language' on children's language acquisition. Among the Ura, babytalk is even used as a term for language perceived as 'wrong'.

These attitudes towards children and child language are comparable to what Casillas et al. (2020a) report for Rossel Islanders and suggest a similar interpretation. While the socio-economic situation and children's chore curriculum are typical for non-Western, subsistence-based societies, the community members emphasise that it is important to talk with children. Parents' ideologies towards child language socialisation thus does not seem to be an important factor for the small amount of children's linguistic input in Raunsepna. Rather, participant constellation and activity type shape children's language environment.

Part II: Comparison of adult- and child-directed speech

3
Direct comparison of ADS and CDS: The Qaqet pear story corpus

In the following chapters, I present a direct comparison between adult and child-directed speech in Qaqet. An elicited narrative task was used to control for the content of the speakers' communications. Each adult told the same story twice, once to an adult and once to a child between 28 and 67 months old.

These narrations were videotaped, transcribed and annotated on various levels. The transcripts were then analysed for features that are known to vary between CDS and ADS: mean length of utterance (Chapter 4), disfluencies (Chapter 5), prosodic features (Chapter 6), speech acts (Chapter 7), corrective input (Chapter 8) and the lexicon (Chapter 9). Section 3.1 describes the methods, while Section 3.2 is dedicated to the data.

3.1 Methods of data collection

The present section is dedicated to the methodology of the comparative study. Section 3.1.1 introduces the pear film as a stimulus. In Section 3.1.2 the sampling and selection of participants is explained, the data collection methods are introduced and some challenges, along with their solutions, are presented.

3.1.1 The stimulus

The stimulus chosen for this study is the 'pear film' (Chafe 1980). The pear film is a video of approximately six minutes produced by Chafe et al. in 1975. It was designed to allow for cross-linguistic comparison of different people talking about the very same topic. Its content (see below for the complete summary as given by Chafe) is easy to interpret for people from different cultural backgrounds, and the film does not contain any language.

Chafe and colleagues (1980) used the stimulus successfully with people with such diverse language backgrounds as English in California, Chinese in Taipei, Japanese in Tokyo, Malay in northern Malaysia, Thai in Bangkok, Persian in Tehran, Greek in Athens, German in Berlin, Creole in Haiti, and K'iche' and Sacapultec in Guatemala.

I chose the pear film as a stimulus because the villagers expressed great interest in videos during my first stay in Raunsepna in 2015, and asked me to bring some with me on my next visit. Showing the film thus promised to result in the relatively natural setting of someone telling somebody else about something interesting (albeit unusual) they had experienced during the day: 'people's mental processing of films appears in various ways to approach the processing of "reality"' (Chafe 1980: xii). Additionally, telling bedtime stories is a common cultural practice in Raunsepna. In example (28) from Hellwig (2020) a grandmother describes how the children tell the stories to their friends afterwards:

(28) *Ide resiit nanget de dama renngi aris. [...] Deip maget, de sa nyitlirang ngatit. De sa irang ngeresiit, naluqa amasiitka, imedu iani, de ngerenarliqa. [...] Tika amasiitka qatit. Sa qatira, mrama.. ama.. amaburlem nara. Be radrlem luqa amasiitka.*
'They (the parents) used to tell them (stories) at night. [...] Then later you will right away see the little ones (children) go around. And they will right away tell this (same) story (to their friends), the (story) that they have just heard. [...] And so the story spreads. It now spreads to many (people). And they now know the story, too.'

The incentive to pass the story on to his older brother was also used during the recordings for the comparative corpus by a mother to motivate her son to listen (see (29)).

(29) *Itnani qukun de nyisil barek ma S.*
      'Afterwards you go to tell the story to S.'

Apart from these ecological advantages, I appreciated the possibility of broad cross-linguistic comparison a widely used stimulus like the pear film would allow.

To comprehend the analyses in the next sections, it will be useful to know the 'pear film story'. Chafe (1980) describes it like this:

> The film begins with a man picking pears on a ladder in a tree. He descends the ladder, kneels, and dumps the pears from the pocket of an apron he is wearing into one of three baskets below the tree. He removes a bandana from around his neck and wipes off one of the pears. Then he returns to the ladder and climbs back into the tree.
>
> Toward the end of this sequence we hear the sound of a goat, and when the picker is back in the tree a man approaches with a goat on a leash. As they pass by the baskets of pears, the goat strains toward them, but it is pulled past by the man and the two of them disappear in the distance.
>
> We see another closeup of the picker at his work, and then we see a boy approaching on a bicycle. He coasts toward the baskets, stops, gets off his bike, looks up at the picker, puts down his bike, walks toward the baskets, again looking and the picker, picks up a pear, puts it back down, looks once more at the picker, and lifts up a basket full of pears. He puts the basket down near his bike, lifts up the bike and straddles it, picks up the basket and places it on the rack in front of his handlebars, and rides off. We again see the man continuing to pick pears.
>
> The boy is now riding down the road, and we see a pear fall from the basket on his bike. Then we see a girl on a bicycle approaching from the other direction. As they pass, the boy turns to look at the girl, his hat flies off, and the front wheel of his bike hits a rock. The bike falls over, the basket falls off, and the pears spill out onto the ground. The boy extricates himself from under the bike, and brushes off his leg.
>
> In the meantime we hear what turns out to be the sound of a paddleball, and then we see three boys standing there, looking at the bike boy on the ground. The three pick up the scattered pears and put them back in the basket. The bike boy sets his bike

upright, and two of the other boys lift the basket of pears back onto it. The bike boy begins walking his bike in the direction he was going, while the three other boys begin walking off in the other direction. As they walk by the bike boy's hat on the road, the boy with the paddleball sees it, picks it up, turns around, and we hear a loud whistle as he signals to the bike boy. The bike boy stops, takes three pears out of the basket, and holds them out as the other boy approaches with the hat. They exchange the pears and the hat, and the bike boy keeps going while the boy with the paddleball runs back to his two companions, to each of whom he hands a pear. They continue on, eating their pears.

The scene now changes back to the tree, where we see the picker again descending the ladder. He looks at the two baskets, where earlier there were three, points at them, backs up against the ladder, shakes his head, and tips up his hat. The three boys are now seen approaching, eating their pears. The picker watches them pass by, and they walk off into the distance. (Chafe 1980: xiii)

3.1.2 Participants, procedure and challenges

The data for the pear stories were collected and transcribed with the help of community members in 2016 and 2017. I targeted people as participants with children between 24 and 48 months of age to allow for comparisons with the longitudinal data in our project.

Typically, in small communities, sampling is a challenging procedure (Schilling-Estes 2013: 31). As Kelly et al. (2015: 291) note, communities that speak lesser known languages are often rather small, which can make it difficult to get the appropriate sample size:

> While families are interested and in some cases eager to participate, cultural practices and traditions take precedence and dictate their movement in ways that may be in conflict with the needs of the research project.

This study is based on a convenience sample for which a range of criteria have been applied. Each narrator tells the story twice: once to an adult, and once to a child. The adult listener is a spouse, close relative or friend. The children are either the narrator's own offspring, or they are sufficiently familiar with them to allow for a convenient experimental situation. An equal number of women and men function as narrators. It was not always possible to determine the exact age of the children beforehand.

3. DIRECT COMPARISON OF ADS AND CDS

Hence, the age of the children was occasionally misinterpreted, and the age of the children participating can be as high as 67 months, even though 48 months was the desired maximum age.

In order to ensure a high degree of control over the situation, I wanted only the narrator and the addressee present. In practice, this setting does not prevail in Raunsepna: people spend most of their time in groups with a varying number of children around. So usually, several adults would arrive for the recordings, accompanied by their children and their children's friends. Sending them away seemed inappropriate, as also described by Du Bois (1980: 6): 'Forcing the speaker to isolate herself from her family would probably have injected an alien tension into an otherwise relatively natural setting'. This resulted in various mixed-participant settings with multiple speakers co-constructing the story, which is the usual way of storytelling in Raunsepna (Hellwig personal communication). Those recordings were only included in the data analysis if the roles of narrator and listener were still predominantly fulfilled by the persons who were meant to do so.

After the arrival of the participants and some acclimatisation, I explained the procedure. One of the participants would watch a film on the laptop, while the other one, or the child, would wait outside. Then I set up the camera and the other person was called back. I went outside while the person who watched the film told the other about what happened in the video. There were no constraints regarding the manner of retelling apart from it being done in Qaqet and in such a way that the listener could make sense of it. The listener could interrupt the narration at any time to ask questions. Participants were explicitly asked to narrate in Qaqet, as this is the dominant language in Raunsepna and the language everyone uses when talking to their children (Marley 2013). This instruction was necessary as some speakers offered to talk in their lingua franca, Tok Pisin, to facilitate understanding for me. Usually, the participants had some questions concerning my expectations, which I answered as much as possible without revealing the actual target of the experiment. Some wanted to know if they would have to remember every detail of the film or if there would be a test concerning its content. Many were interested in the names of the fruits, how they should refer to them in the narration and how they would be prepared for a meal.

When there were two adults present, they discussed who would be the narrator and who the listener. However, if one of them had already told the story to a child, he or she was asked to tell the story again. I hoped that this way, those participants who felt more comfortable telling stories would be the ones to narrate. Especially in the case of the younger children (36 months and below, i.e. the first year of the age range I aimed for), opinions regarding the ability of the child to listen and comprehend the story were always discussed previously with his or her caregivers, not with the intent to exclude them from the study but rather to encourage some discussion about storytelling with children. In the case of the older children, it was assumed that they would be able to follow the narration. What the participants estimated did not have a clear relation to the age of the children but rather reflected quite accurately the subsequent behaviour of the child: if the parents had doubts concerning the ability of the child to listen, the child usually turned out to be lacking in concentration. If the parents were optimistic about the whole situation, usually the children were interested, engaged and interacted vividly with the narrator. A challenge to a controlled experimental situation was that many children watched the film along with the narrators and it was not possible to send them away. Accordingly, the CDS-stories are often built on the narrators' assumption of a shared watching experience whereas the ADS-stories are not. It cannot be ruled out that the shared experience influenced the style of narration, but obvious differences other than occasional questions like, 'Did you see that, too?', posed to children, were not detected.

Another obstacle was that as soon as there were adults or older children present, people did not address the narration to the young children with the narration any more. This hints at a situation-centred style of caregiving as described for many non-Western communities by Schieffelin and Ochs (1986). Children are not positioned at the centre of attention, but they accompany adults during their everyday activities and thereby adapt to observational learning (see Chapter 2).

All the narrations were videotaped with a Zoom Q8 recorder plus internal microphone in a MOV/WAV format (1080/30). Recording times had to be chosen carefully, especially to avoid a noisy environment (Crowley & Thieberger 2010: 124), as the setup was hardly protected from ambient noise like afternoon rains or noisy garden work.

For most of the challenges, it was possible to find compromises. Still, I definitely lost 'some of the control which is sought after by Western scientists, but this seemed preferable to imposing an alien way and receiving stilted and unnatural narratives in turn' (DuBois 1980: 7).

Altogether, 48 stories were collected and transcribed, but only 20 stories were chosen for statistical comparison (displayed in Table 3.2 and 3.3). Stories told by siblings (13) were excluded as beyond the scope of this study, other stories were excluded from the study for various reasons (see Table 3.1; one particular reason may apply to more than one story).

Table 3.1: Reasons for the exclusion of collected stories.

Reason for exclusion	Stories excluded
There were two adult speakers present	5
There was no CDS-story for comparison	3
There was no ADS-story for comparison	2
The child was too old	1
The audio quality was too bad due to heavy rain	1
The narrator told another story than the pear story	1
The child cried all the time	1
The older siblings joined in storytelling	1
The whole family was present, the young child was not addressed	1

3.2 The data

In Section 3.2.1 I will introduce the corpus, then explain the transcription and coding process (Section 3.2.2). In Section 3.2.3 the different tiers in the examples are introduced. Following this, I will present the segmentation conventions with regard to intonation units (Section 3.2.4) and words (Section 3.2.5).

3.2.1 The corpus

Altogether, 20 pear stories were selected for the comparison of features. Table 3.2 shows background data for the CDS-corpus and 3.3 for the ADS corpus. Mean age of the speakers is 36.7 years, for the adult listeners 34.7 years, and for the children 44.3 months, but as can be seen from Table 3.2 and Table 3.3, there is a large amount of variation. For the children, due to the large variation in age, the results from different age groups will occasionally be addressed separately in the remainder of this work. For each speaker, an ADS and a CDS version is available. The CDS part of the corpus consists of 1,178 intonation units (6,754 words), the

ADS-part of 1,049 intonation units (7,511 words). Altogether the corpus has a size of 2,227 intonation units (14,265 words). Each participant told the story twice. In the sample selected for comparison, half of the stories, both ADS and CDS, are first retellings and half are second retellings. This was meant to distribute the effects of the repetition across the two conditions.

Table 3.2: CDS-pear data: speaker code (ID), age, sex and relationships of participants.

ID	Age (y)	Sex	Chi1	Age (m)	Sex	Chi2	Age (m)	Sex	Relationship Speaker/Chi
ABD	36	f	XCL	33	m	ZGT	72	m	mother
AGK	28	f	WMM	53	f	-	-	-	aunt
ALR	40	f	XMU	60	f	-	-	-	mother
AMT	25	f	YDS	36	f	YRA	51	m	mother
ARL	37	m	XAT	34	m	-	-	-	father
AVD	32	m	YMN	40	f	-	-	-	father
BCP	40	m	XRN	40	f	-	-	-	father
BLN	31	f	ZDL	28	m	-	-	-	mother
DCK	39	m	ZEA	34	f	-	-	-	father
DCM	59	m	XEB	67	f	-	-	-	grandfather

As can be seen in Table 3.2, older children were present in two narrations. For ZGT, this did not seem problematic as ABD still directed her speech to the primary listener XCL, as was apparent from her gaze and gestures. YRA's presence was not a problem as he was within the focal age range of the current study anyway. For the statistics on MLU (Chapter 4), disfluencies (Chapter 5) and prosodic features (Chapter 6), the mean age of the listening children has been used for correlations with age. In the section about interaction (Chapter 7), the age of the child originally intended as addressee is used as many of the speech acts under investigation serve to attain the attention of the relevant child.

In the CDS story told by ARL, his wife and the mother of XAT is also present, but watches quietly most of the time. She starts to interfere only once during the story, but she is mostly ignored by ARL. Her data have been included in the analysis only in Chapter 9, as she is the only adult producing specific baby talk words.

3. DIRECT COMPARISON OF ADS AND CDS

Table 3.3: ADS-pear data: speaker code (ID), age, sex and relationships of participants.

ID	Age (y)	Sex	Listener	Age (y)	Sex	Relationship Speaker/Hearer
ABD	36	f	XCS	12	f	mother
AGK	28	f	AMM	25	f	neighbour
ALR	40	f	ACL	61	f	neighbour
AMT	25	f	AHL	29	m	wife
ARL	37	m	ACP	38	m	neighbour
AVD	32	m	AMM	25	f	husband
BCP	40	m	ARN	34	f	husband
BLN	31	f	APA	34	m	wife
DCK	39	m	AJK	approx. 35	m	neighbour
DCM	59	m	AMI	54	f	husband

The choice of 12-year-old XCS as listener in the ADS-corpus is based on the fact that so far, the features that discriminate CDS from ADS are only found in the speech directed at young children. Significant differences have been previously reported, for example by Snow (1972), when comparing speech to toddlers with speech to six year olds. Twelve year olds, who also fulfill many adult duties in Raunsepna, can therefore be expected to be spoken to in language typical for ADS. There was high individual variation in how much interaction there was between child and narrator, as can be seen from Table 3.4.

Table 3.4: Utterance and word counts in the CDS-stories.

Speaker	U/CDS	W/CDS	Child	U/Child	W/Child
ABD	116	611	ZCL	3	9
AGK	153	1015	WMM	0	0
ALR	93	658	XMU	13	13
AMT	85	474	YDS	21	40
ARL	124	485	XAT	77	204
AVD	71	412	YMN	27	49
BCP	145	1096	XRN	8	8
BLN	124	526	ZDL	62	85
DCK	150	630	ZEA	11	11
DCM	117	847	XEB	14	40

Some children like ZDL, XAT, YMN and YDS interacted intensely with their parent while they were told the story. Others did not talk at all (WMM), or hardly spoke and were barely understandable (ZEA). This is partly due to the expectations of the parents: some, like BLN, made a great effort to have their child join them in telling the story. Hellwig (2020) describes co-construction stories with children as the normal social practice in Raunsepna. Others, like AVD in example (30), suppressed their children's conversational turns. AVD clearly emphasises that it is him, not his daughter YMN, who is supposed to talk.

(30) *sung nanyi de ngusiit banyi*
      sung   ne-nyi   de
      quiet   from/with-2sg   CONJ
      ngu=siit   barek-nyi
      1SG.SBJ.NPST=tell_story   BEN-2SG
      'be quiet so I can tell you the story' (PearAVDP 005)

Still, this does not explain all the differences: DCK, for example, tried very hard to make his daughter ZEA speak without much success, while AVD's daughter was not impressed at all by his attempts to have her listen quietly and instead continued imitating what he said. When explaining the task, I tried to make it clear to all parents that they should narrate the story in such a way that the child would understand it. The results still reflect their own, culturally mediated, interpretations of appropriate behaviour in an experimental situation like the one I created.

For all pear stories, only the part where the story is actually told is counted for analysis: most speakers explicitly signalled the beginning and end of the story. The surrounding material, mostly clarification of the task among the speakers, was excluded from analysis. Only if off-topic scenes occur within the storytelling are they taken into account for the analysis.

3.2.2 Transcription and coding

Once the story had been recorded, I segmented and transcribed it with community members. If non-participants who were helping with the transcription were not able to understand what was said in the video, the original participants were asked. This was especially helpful in the case of unintelligible child utterances, as mothers and fathers could usually tell what the child said or, at least, intended to say.

Before every transcription session of CDS-stories I asked the transcribers to pay special attention to speech they perceived to be typical for speech directed to children. This happened only once, during transcription of the story told by ARL to his son XAT (see Chapter 9).

For the transcribers, it was especially challenging not to correct people when they judged the Qaqet utterances to deviate from what they perceived as correct language. It reassured them, however, that I always wrote a corrected version, too, which would allow me to identify children's non-target-like productions. The Qaqet version, as repeated by the speakers in the transcription sessions, and a free Tok Pisin translation were written into notebooks and checked when digitised in the evening. I marked all doubtful sequences where the audio/video data and the written version seemed to differ from each other, and verified them with community members.

The transcribed stories were then transferred to ELAN, exported to Toolbox and interlinearised. Once interlinearised, the data were transferred back to ELAN where a tier following the CHAT (Codes for the Human Analysis of Transcripts) annotation conventions (MacWhinney 2000) was created for the inclusion of features like hesitations, self-interruptions and special forms. An additional tier for the annotation of speech acts was also created. The exact coding decisions, if necessary, will be discussed in the relevant chapters. The various levels of annotation are shown here in the example format.

3.2.3 Example format and pitch display

In the Qaqet pear corpus, there are various levels of analysis, see (31):[1]

(31) (a) *masmasna retatnavet luqa*
    (b) masmasna   te=tatna=pet
    (c) quickly:redupl   3pl.sbj=do_work:recp=on/under
        lu-ka-a d
        em-nc.sg.m-dist
    (d) 'quickly they help him' (PearALRA 092)

In line (a), the original text is given as dictated by the transcribers, and written down and edited by me with help of community members. The text separated by blanks corresponds largely to phonological words. For representation of hesitation pauses or self-interruptions, '..' is used.

1   The tier following the CHAT-conventions (MacWhinney 2000) is not included in the examples.

Line (b) of (31) shows the morpheme break as generated with the help of the program Field Linguist's Toolbox (SIL 2018 [2002]).[2] Line (c) contains the interlinearisation following the Leipzig Glossing Rules. In line (d), a free English translation is provided.

Speech is presented graphically through periograms (Albert et al. 2020), which is a novel way of displaying pitch, modulated with periodic energy, hence pitch intelligibility (Oxenham 2012), with the aim of creating a 'perceptually motivated representation of the pitch contour of an utterance' (Albert et al. 2018: 807). The workflow is described in Albert et al. (2018) and uses the Praat script mausoooth (Cangemi 2015) for extraction, manual inspection, smoothing and interpolation of F0 trajectories in Praat (Boersma & Weenink 2021). Periograms are then created in R (R Core Team 2018) with ggplot (Wickham 2009), whereby periodic energy is represented through the transparency and width of the line. I opted for displaying pitch in semitones (st) rather than Herz (Hz) with a fixed pitch range window of 20 st to allow for maximum comparability across gender and across speaking style. The resulting periograms hence offer a highly information-rich and, most importantly, perceptually based representation of speech.

3.2.4 Segmentation: Intonation units

It is of great relevance to apply consistent criteria to identify utterance boundaries, especially if one wishes to study utterance-related topics like the mean length of utterance (MLU), or annotate features, such as speech acts, at the utterance-level (Rowe 2012: 202).

In this section, these criteria will be outlined. The unit of segmentation chosen here is the intonation unit (IU) as:

> It is widely held to be the basic unit into which native speakers themselves chunk their utterances, i.e. it is seen as a unit of speech production which in some sense has a psychological reality for the speakers as opposed to a purely analytic construct 'invented' by linguists. (Himmelmann 2006: 260)

Chafe characterises intonation units as each containing one single focus of consciousness:

---

2   A dictionary and a parsing database for Qaqet, on which I could draw for interlinearisation, were developed by Birgit Hellwig.

> It is intuitively satisfying to suppose that each intonation unit verbalizes the information active in the speaker's mind at its onset. (Chafe 1994: 63)

Accordingly, it makes sense to assume that it is also a real unit for the hearer, that is, conceptualised in such a way by the speaker that it is what he wants to present to his hearer as one single 'focus of consciousness'.

One intonation unit is identified by its coherent pitch contour. Intonation units may be, but do not have to be, divided by pauses. Of course, there is variation between languages in the form of those contours. The Qaqet patterns as described by Hellwig (2019) are listed in Table 3.5.

Table 3.5: Intonation contours in Qaqet (Hellwig 2019: 56).

Type	Prosody	Function
Final	final fall	declarative utterance; final member of a list
Non-final	final rise-fall	non-final unit of a declarative utterance (e.g., non-final clause, left-dislocated constituent, interjection *kuasik* 'no' and vocative); possibly also some phrasal units
Continuation	final level	self-interruption; introducing reported
	+ glottalisation	speech and non-verbal demonstrations
List	final rise	non-final member of a list
Content question	fall	interrogative (content question)
Quoted content	initial rise	reported interrogative (content question)
question	+ final fall	
Polar question	final rise-fall	interrogative (polar question)
Imperative	(initial rise) + final rise	imperative

Most of the contours in Table 3.5 pose no problems in segmentation, as each contour exemplifies a full intonation unit. However, additional criteria for segmentation have to be employed for the continuation type:

'Speakers interrupt utterances when searching for words or continuations. In such cases, the pitch level is held and the last word is uttered with final glottalization' (Hellwig 2019: 61). Usually after those intonation units, a pause occurs. After the pause, there are two possibilities, and segmentation in the current corpus depends on the continuation of the intonation pattern. If there is a reset in pitch after the pause, the pause is interpreted as a case of self-interruption and is then delimited an intonation unit. If the intonation pattern is continued, the pause is interpreted as a hesitation pause (Himmelmann 2014: 935). Thus the material before and after the pause is analysed as one single intonation unit, and is not segmented separately.

Example (32) and Figure 3.1 show a typical hesitation pause and its intonation contour. The article *ama* is uttered before the hesitation pause and repeated after it. Before the pause, it shows final glottalisation and carries level pitch. The intonation contour is not interrupted, but stays steady until the end where it shows a rise-fall. In this case, the material before and after the hesitation pause is not segmented separately but analysed as one single intonation unit.

(32)   *katrama.. amaningara*
       ka=tat   ama   ama=ninga-it-a
       3SG.M.SBJ=take   ART   ART=head-NC.SG.LONG-DIST
       'he takes the.. the cap' (PearALRA 107)

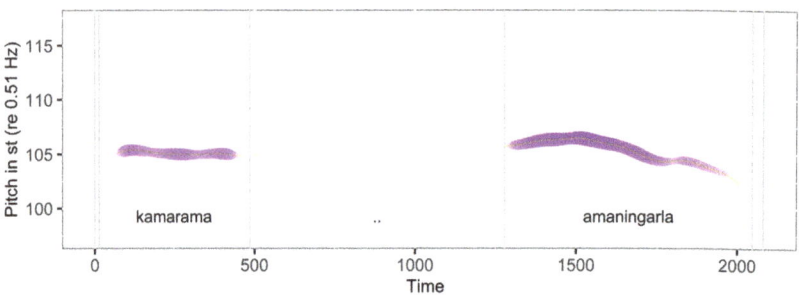

Figure 3.1: F₀-extraction for (32) (female speaker).

Example (33) with Figure 3.2 shows a typical self-interruption. The intonation contour is interrupted after *de* and restarted after the hesitation pause. The *de* is glottalised and involves a jump in pitch of nearly 100Hz. The boundary between the two intonation units thus occurs between *de* and *tatit*.

(33)   *deiva de.. tatit dera..*
       de=ip-a   de   ta=tit   de=ta
       conj=conj-dist   conj   3pl.sbj=go   conj=3pl.sbj
       'and then.. they go and they..' (PearARLA 105/106)

I applied Himmelmann's (2014: 936) suggestion that pauses above 500msec lead to abandonment of the original intonation contour because speakers usually cannot continue it. Random acoustical analyses confirmed that this was a good approximation. Therefore, those strings of speech have been segmented separately unless it was clearly audible that the intonation contour continued. The reliability was tested with the help of one student trained in segmentation according to intonation units. She re-segmented four randomly chosen stories, half CDS and half ADS. This resulted in 95 per cent accordance between my own segmentations and hers for CDS and 78 per cent for ADS.

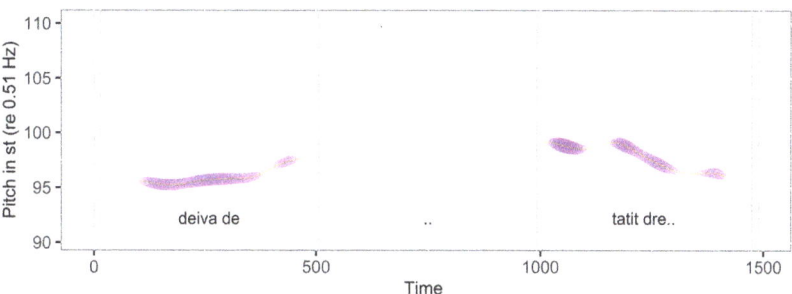

Figure 3.2: F0-extraction for (33) (male speaker).

3.2.5 Segmentation: Words and clitics

In this section, the segmentation of words in the corpus is explained. The differentiation is important for word counts and calculations of MLU. A clitic (without its host) is counted as a full word, whereas a suffix counts as a word only together with its host. This decision is based on the criteria proposed by Zwicky and Pullum (1983), explained by Spencer and Luís (2012), and applied to Qaqet by Hellwig (2019) with some additional criteria. Hellwig invokes three arguments for the analysis of a given formative in Qaqet, either as a clitic or as a suffix:

1. **Selectivity with regard to its host:** suffixes are strict, whereas clitics attach to a range of forms.
2. **Morphophonological idiosyncrasies:** suffixes may show phonological changes or trigger them in the stems to which they are attached, changes 'that are not the result of completely regular phonological processes that affect all words or words combinations of a given phonological type' (Spencer & Luís 2012: 109).
3. **Word-like appearance:** occurrence as free morpheme or indications of word boundaries before the realisation of a clitic.

Qaqet shows extensive cliticisation. The difference between cliticisation and affixation can be illustrated with the help of free subject pronouns and pronominal suffixes, both of which index arguments on the verb. As explained by Hellwig, the pronominal suffixes are analysed as such because:

> they invariably form a phonological word with the preceding preposition or verb. Qaqet clitics, by contrast, are more variable: the same form can usually be realized as either a proclitic or an enclitic, depending on the environment. And second, the pronominal arguments trigger phonological changes in preceding elements that are otherwise only attested in suffixes, not in enclitics. (Hellwig 2019: 107)

Example (34) shows an instance of the subject clitic *ke* '3SG.M.SBJ.NPST' realised as a proclitic.

(34) *tika luqa **q**eksiqa [...]*
 tika lu-ka-a **ke**=ksik-a
 EMPH DEM-NC.SG.M-DIST 3SG.M.SBJ.NPST=climb-DIST
 'it is that the other man climbs [...]' (PearARLA 025)

In example (35), in contrast, the subject clitic *ta* '3pl.sbj' appears in enclitic position.

(35) *tatramagama ndsaqi**ra**..*
 ta=tat ama=gam-a
 3PL.SBJ=take/pick_up ART=seed/fruit-DIST
 de=saqi=**ta**
 CONJ=again/also=3PL.SBJ
 'they pick the fruits and they..' (PearARLA 070)

The realisation of subject pronominals as proclitic in (34) and as enclitic in (35) shows their openness to attach to a range of different forms, and supports their analysis as clitics. Similarly, the next two examples show how the suffix pronouns may cause morphological idiosyncrasies. In (36), the word *kuarl* 'give' appears in its standard form, whereas in (37), the combination with the suffix *-ta* '3pl.h' triggers the appearance of the *a* between the two forms.

(36) *katira bequkuarl luqa*
 ka=tit-a   be=ke=kuarl
 3SG.M.SBJ=go-DIST CONJ=3SG.M.SBJ.NPST=present/shine
 luka-a
 DEM-NC.SG.M-DIST
 'he goes and he gives it to this man' (PearARLA 098)

(37) *kukuarlara araagam amadepguas*
 ke=kuarl-ta   araa=gam
 3SG.M.SBJ.NPST=present/shine-3PL.H 3PL.POSS=seed/fruit
 ama=depguas
 ART=three
 'he gives them their three fruits' (PearAGKP 136)

The third of the three criteria above, namely the word-like appearance, can be explained with reference to the demonstratives. They consist of a base *lu*, a noun class suffix (e.g. *-a* 'dist' or *-iara* 'prox') and a deictic root. However, the situation is slightly different for *mara* 'here'. Occasionally, it is realised as a separate word, therefore it is analysed as an enclitic (Hellwig 2019: 201ff.). The determiners, too, are analysed as clitics rather than prefixes, since they can occur as free morphemes or form a clitic group with the preceding preposition instead of the following noun (Hellwig 2019: 118).

The three criteria applied here align clitics with words rather than with affixes. Accordingly, I decided to include clitics into the word counts whereas an affix and its host count as one word. This will be of relevance in Chapter 4 on the mean length of utterances.

4
Mean length of utterance

In this chapter, I compare the mean length of utterances (henceforth MLU) in Qaqet CDS and ADS. Section 4.1 summarises previous research on mean length of utterance in CDS. Then in Section 4.2 the definition of an utterance and its operationalisation for the calculation of the MLU in Qaqet are discussed. Afterwards, in Section 4.3 the choice of words over morphemes as a measure of utterance length is explained. Finally, in Section 4.4, the methodology is introduced and the results for MLU in the Qaqet pear corpus are presented.

4.1 Previous research on MLU in CDS

The MLU is a measure used to assess syntactic complexity, both in child language development and in caregiver speech (Snow 1972; Harkness 1977). Reduced complexity in CDS is associated with ease of comprehension. Brown (1973) first used the measure for assessing the language competence of English children, assuming that every step in development, associated with complexity, increases length (1973: 53). He proposed five stages of development, ranging from 1.75 morphemes per utterance to 4.00. MLU measures exceeding four morphemes per utterance have been found not to be representative of other developmental features (Behrens 2008).

Various studies show that CDS has a lower MLU than ADS. The MLU count has been criticised because it may 'mask utterance-by-utterance changes in the complexity of the speech which mothers address to their children' (Pine 1994: 18). It has nevertheless proven a valuable measure for the analysis of CDS.

Snow (1972) found in her experiments that the MLU of English-speaking mothers' speech to 10 year olds was higher (10.9–11.2 words) than when speaking to two-year-old children (6.6–9.8 words). Newport et al. (1977) tested the speech of English-speaking mothers to children aged 12–27 months and their utterances proved significantly shorter (4.3 words) than the speech directed at the experimenter (11.9 words). Phillips (1973) found in her experiments that the utterances of English mothers speaking to children of eight months (3.6 words), 18 months (3.5 words) and 28 months (4.0 words) were significantly shorter than when speaking to adults (8.45 words).

Regarding research on non-Indo-European languages spoken in less WEIRD environments, there is some variation. Pye (1986a) did not discover differences in Mayan mothers' MLU whether they were talking to children or adults.[1] He attributes this to the effect of cultural concepts, as children are not usually addressed in K'iche', but also considers personality and speech style as possible factors (Pye 1986a: 92). Vaughan et al. (2015) measured the caregivers' MLU in naturalistic recordings at two distinct points of time for two Australian Kriols. They discovered, for Wumpurrarni English in Tennant Creek, that the caregiver's MLU increases as children grow older, but the opposite happens in the Fitzroy Valley Kriol-speaking community in Yakanarra. The authors explain these differences in part with reference to the small sample size and the different age range of the child participants in the two communities. For CDS in Australian Pitjantjatjara, Defina (2020) reported a lower MLU than in ADS, increasing gradually with child age. Such a correlation with children's age or the children's MLU suggests that adults adapt their speech to the age of children, which is well known from a study of CDS in large-scale societies (Phillips 1973; Newport et al. 1977). Ko (2012) reports that the MLU of British and American English-speaking mothers

---

[1] Research on other Mayan languages reports that there is no register of speech for small children, especially as they are infrequently addressed by caregivers (Pfeiler 2007). Despite the vast body of literature on acquisition of Mayan languages, I was not able to find other studies on MLU of CDS in Mayan languages.

does not increase in a linear fashion but rather shows abrupt shifts correlating with milestones in the children's development, such as the start of word combinations. However, the data did not allow for conclusions regarding the causal direction of this correlation. The reported literature has shown that in many languages, MLU in CDS is lower, but increases with age, and that ideologies towards child language socialisation may be of relevance. In Section 2.2.4, I reported that a low utterance length is seen by Qaqet mothers as beneficial for successful communication with children. Therefore, I expect to find a low MLU in speech to smaller children that increases with child age.

First, the MLU of CDS and ADS are compared. In order to test if the MLU in CDS depends on the maturation of the child, the MLU of CDS was correlated with child age. The latter was taken as a proxy for the development of the child.

Before proceeding to the analysis of the data, the following basic difficulty must be addressed:

> In order to compute a MLU, one has to decide what is a word and what is an utterance and these are two of the biggest decisions that one has to make when transcribing and analyzing child language. In this sense, the computation of MLU serves as a methodological trip wire for the consideration of these two deeper issues. (MacWhinney 2000: 57)

This is addressed in the next two sections. The concepts of utterance and word are defined and operationalised based on the literature on MLU while also considering the specifics of Qaqet grammar.

4.2 Utterances

In the following, I will define and operationalise the concept of 'utterance' with regard to literature on MLU, the way others have operationalised it, and to the Qaqet pear corpus. In this study, I take an utterance to be the smallest unit carrying communicative intention (Tomasello 2009: 72). The intonation unit is equated with the utterance. According to Himmelmann (2006: 270), however, an utterance is a unit on a hierarchically higher level than the intonation unit, made up of intonation units that 'belong closer together' (2006: 270) than others.

There are two questions that arise from these considerations. First, what is the usual definition of utterance in the multiplicity of studies that use MLU as a measure of complexity? Second, what is the relationship between an utterance and an intonation unit in Qaqet?

Most studies do not explicitly define an utterance (Brown 1973; Harkness 1977; Newport et al. 1977). Those studies that do define it use different combinations of criteria. For example, Snow (1972) used phonetic cues, pauses and intonation patterns as indicators for utterance boundaries. The instructions in the CHAT (Codes for the Human Analysis of Transcripts) annotation conventions state that one utterance should not include multiple main clauses and may also consist of incomplete sentences (MacWhinney 2000: 59). The basic utterance terminators in CHAT, like the question mark, the period and the exclamation point, are defined with reference to their intonation contours in English. Still, the comma as a non-terminative symbol is allowed in the CHAT format and expresses 'a combination of features such as pause, syntactic juncture, intonational drop, and others' (MacWhinney 2000: 61). A mixture of syntactic and intonational criteria is used here for identification of utterance boundaries.

Ko remarks in her comparative analysis of 25 corpora from the CHILDES (CHIld Language Data Exchange System) database that this may well lead to 'some differences in the exact method of aligning the utterance boundaries among the transcribers for each of the corpora' (Ko 2012: 845). Miller (1981: 14) counts a terminal intonation contour or a pause of two or three seconds as criterial to identify an utterance boundary, as opposed to the pragmatic criteria proposed by Tomasello (2009) above. Vaughan et al. (2015: 7) merely say about utterances that they can 'range from a single token to a full clause'. Overall, a mix of syntactic, prosodic and pragmatic criteria are applied in the studies that make use of MLU as a measure of syntactic complexity. Clearly, the absence of a common definition affects the comparability of results.

The Qaqet pear corpus is segmented on the basis of prosodic cues (see Section 3.2.4). Instead of applying additional criteria, I used those as unit of comparison. As a means of comparison, the IU offers a more solid measure than the varied composition of features applied so far, especially with regard to different languages.

4.3 Words or morphemes?

For the current study, the MLU has been calculated in words. In this section, the use of words versus morphemes as a measure of utterance length is discussed. Brown (1973) argued for the use of morphemes (MLUm) instead of words for calculating the mean length of child utterances because many new developments in child language are mirrored in the addition of new morphemes (1973: 53f). Subsequently, both variants have been used in many studies. For CDS, Snow (1972) and Harkness (1977) as well as Ko (2012) used words as a basic unit. For Ko, this decision was motivated by the fact that not all the corpora in her cross-linguistic examination contained a morpheme break line. Allen and Dench (2015) tested the different measures, and calculated the MLU for eastern Canadian Inuktitut child utterances in words (MLUw), in morphemes (MLUm) and in syllables (MLUs). They additionally counted the mean length of words in morphemes (MLWm) and syllables (MLWs). They found that only the MLUm, MLWm and MLWs correlated significantly with the age of the children and could thus serve as a reliable predictor of the language ability of the children. Inuktitut is a polysynthetic language with a rich inflectional system. What is considered a word could be made up of 11 morphemes or more (Allen & Dench 2015: 379). Therefore, it is not surprising that words per utterance is not a useful measure in this case. Consequently, not only developmental issues, but also the typological profile of a language, must be taken into account when deciding on the units to count in order to calculate the MLU. Qaqet is not a polysynthetic language, but it does make extensive use of cliticisation, resulting in fairly long phonological words. Therefore, the decision was made to calculate the MLU on the basis of grammatical words, that is, both free morphemes and clitics were counted as separate words (while affixes were not counted). Nevertheless, a test with morpheme counts showed that the results of the ADS/CDS-comparison did not significantly change.

4.4 Procedure and results

To calculate the MLU, I used the CLAN (Computerized Language ANalysis) MLU program (MacWhinney 2000). This program runs on the tier annotated with the CHAT annotation format MacWhinney (2000). Brown (1973: 54) proposed a set of rules for calculating the MLU for child language that is still widely applied and partially implemented in the CLAN program. Utterances containing unintelligible words are excluded, and repeated material is not counted. Many of Brown's other rules are designed for English or child language, and will not be considered here. The MLU program needs utterance delimiters (such as a period or a question mark) to identify the boundaries of utterances. In the pear corpus, the utterance delimiters are only used on the tier that is annotated corresponding to the CHAT annotation format and segmented by words. Thus, the MLU program was executed on that tier, and calculated using words as a measure of utterance length. Utterances consisting only of single words like 'yes' or a name have been excluded from the count. They cannot be expressed in a less complicated form, and therefore do not reflect if adults adjust utterance length to the age of their interlocutor as they are narrating. Table 4.1 shows the results of the MLU count.

Table 4.1: Results of MLUw counts ADS vs CDS.

Age, ID	MLUwADS	MLUwCDS
28, BLN	9.950	6.720
34, DCK	7.460	5.300
34, ARL	7.430	5.200
40, AVD	6.960	6.250
40, BCP	8.050	8.000
44, AMT	7.030	6.740
53, ABD	5.270	6.060
53, AGK	7.160	6.730
60, ALR	6.710	7.410
67, DCM	6.980	7.670

The results for CDS and ADS were compared using a Wilcoxon Signed Rank-test for related samples, a test appropriate for small data sets. The samples of CDS (m = 6.6; SD = 0.9) and ADS (m = 7.3, SD = 1.1) did not differ significantly (Z = 9.500; p = 0.066), meaning that the MLU in CDS and ADS is not significantly different. For a visualisation of the results, see Figure 4.1. Each pair of bars represents one speaker. The age of the child she speaks to in months and the speakers' name codes are given on the x-axis. On the y-axis, the MLU in words is shown.

Apart from three speakers, all have a higher MLU in ADS than in CDS.

4. MEAN LENGTH OF UTTERANCE

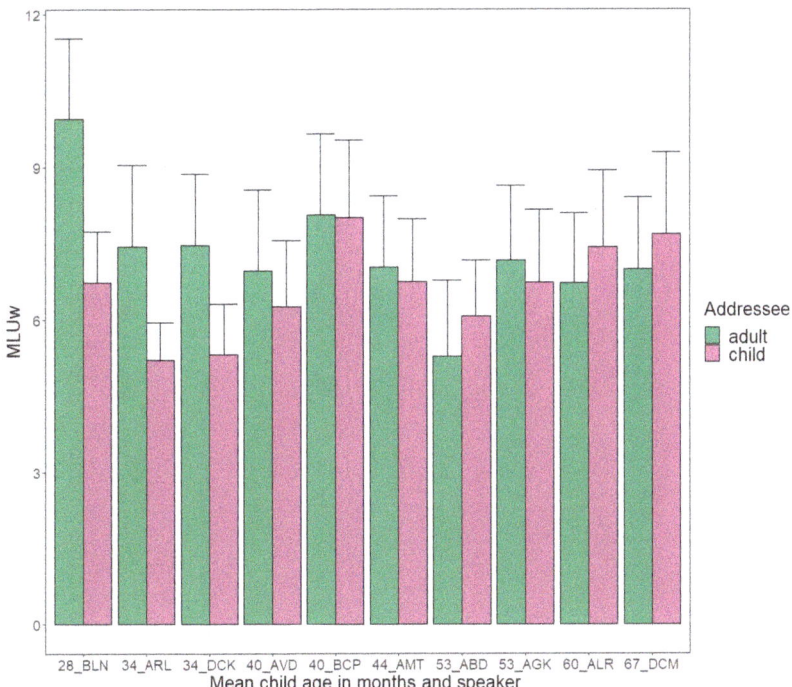

Figure 4.1: MLUw CDS vs MLUw ADS.

From the bars in Figure 4.1, it seems that the difference between ADS utterance length and CDS utterance length gets smaller the older the listening child is. To test if this is a significant effect in the data, the difference in MLUw ADS-CDS was correlated for each individual speaker with the mean age of the listening children. By subtracting the MLUw for CDS from the MLUw for ADS for each speaker, I controlled for the individual differences in utterance length. That value was then correlated with the age of the child involved in the CDS part of the task. In the two cases where two children were present during the CDS task (see Section 3.1.2), their mean age was used. The Spearman coefficient was $r = -0.802$ ($p = 0.005$), the correlation is significant. The results are illustrated in Figure 4.2.

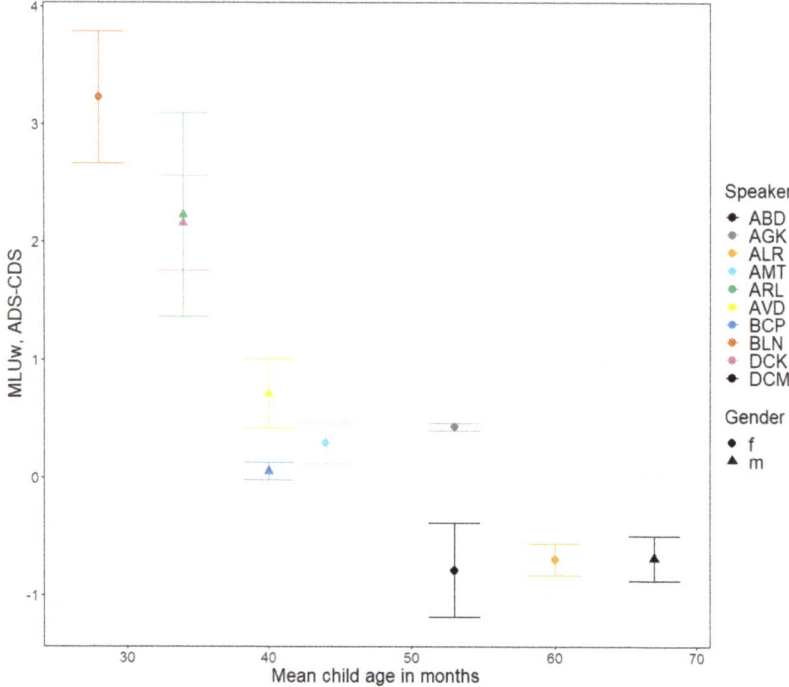

Figure 4.2: MLU(ADS)-MLU(CDS) of individual speakers in correlation with (mean) age of child addressees.

Figure 4.2 shows a clear negative correlation, meaning that the older the child, the smaller the difference gets between CDS and ADS. As hypothesised, the MLU in CDS depends on the age of the child: the older the child, the higher the MLU.

For speakers talking to children up to 36 months of age, the difference in MLU between ADS and CDS is large (mean for ADS is 8.27 words per utterance, and the mean for CDS is 5.74 words per utterance). From Figure 4.2 it can be seen that by around the age of 40 months, there is no difference between ADS and CDS in utterance length any more.

4.5 Summary: MLU in Qaqet CDS

The results show that in the pear story experiment, utterance length in CDS correlates with the age of the children. However, the samples of CDS and ADS do not differ significantly in MLU, probably due to the age of the children in the sample. For children up to the age of 34 months, the MLU is much higher in ADS than in CDS, but approaches ADS-values at around 40 months. In comparison, Defina (2020) found that utterances were still shorter in Pitjantjatjara CDS, for children between three and four years. Harkness (1977) still found significant differences in MLU for Kipsigis CDS at 43 months.

The results also contradict the adults' opinions reported in Section 2.2 that mothers, but not fathers, adapt their speech in communication with child listeners. Qaqet adults' belief that short utterances are easier to understand for small children fits the pattern of age-dependent MLU. Using short utterances can be helpful in communication with children who are not yet fully competent language users. The transition towards more adult-like speech probably reflects adults' perception of the children's growing competence (Harkness 1977; Vaughan et al. 2015).

In this chapter, I used MLU as a measure of complexity for comparison of CDS and ADS in Qaqet. More complicated issues demand more processing effort and may also cause processing difficulties that can result in hesitations. These are addressed in the following chapter.

5
Disfluencies

This chapter deals with disfluencies, in particular, with disfluency pauses. Fluency is one of the features of CDS that has been extensively discussed in the literature. Kidd et al. (2011) describe fluency as one of the 'hallmarks' of CDS. As discussed in Section 1.2, CDS is typically more fluent than ADS (Snow 1996; Broen 1972). In Section 5.1 I will present the types of disfluencies that have already been investigated in studies of CDS in other languages. In Section 5.2, I introduce the types of disfluencies evident in the Qaqet pear corpus, and link them to a model proposed by Clark and Wasow (1998). Unfilled pauses, called disfluency pauses in the following text, are the most common form of disfluency in the data. In Section 3.2.4, I explain their subdivision into hesitation pauses and self-interruptions. In Section 5.3, I will compare disfluency pauses in ADS and CDS in Qaqet, and provide an explanation for the results. Finally, in Section 5.4, in a subcorpus of the pear stories, the positions of hesitations in the sentence will be analysed to investigate whether they occur at positions that may be helpful for the listener, for example, by announcing difficult-to-process linguistic material (Kidd et al. 2011).

5.1 Previous research on disfluencies in CDS

The design of the present study was shaped by several studies that have found fewer disfluencies in CDS than ADS. For example, Broen (1972) showed that the disfluency rates in English differ significantly in speech to adults, speech to children over 45 months, and speech to 18–26-month-old children in a free play condition. The younger the listener, the fewer the disfluencies. For a storytelling condition, the disfluency rates for speech to older and to younger children were comparably low, and both were lower than speech to adults. Thus, as the current study used a narrative condition, it was expected that the rates for speech directed at children over 45 months and under 45 months would both be significantly lower than those in adult-directed speech. Similar evidence, although not for narratives, was provided by Kidd et al. (2011), who investigated disfluencies in CDS data from the CHILDES database. They found a lower rate of hesitation particles than reported in the literature for adult-directed English. Nilsson Björkenstam et al. (2013) showed that there are significantly more disfluencies in ADS than in CDS in their longitudinal recordings of Swedish parent-child interactions with children from six to 33 months. All three studies also stated that the rate of disfluencies increases with the age of the child.

In Section 1.2 it was discussed why a low rate of disfluencies is not a conscious effort to make comprehension easier for the child. The discussion demonstrated that it is improbable that CDS is more fluent *because* the added fluency supports hearers' processing. Instead, it may be the lower complexity, as measured by MLU, that is responsible for the fluency of CDS. Rispoli and Hadley (2001) showed that, for children's productions, sentences with disfluencies tend to be longer and more complex than fluent sentences. Accordingly, in Section 5.3, the length of intonation units with and without hesitations will be compared.

I also presented evidence that hesitations are not necessarily detrimental to comprehension (see Section 1.2). Rather, hesitations occurring before difficult material may even aid listeners by reducing their processing load by announcing complications (Kidd et al. 2011) or relevant boundaries (Snow 1972). The results of those studies suggest that even young children can make use of them and modify their expectations towards following referents accordingly (Kidd et al. 2011). These findings were confirmed by Owens and Graham (2016) for three-year-old children, but not for two year olds. Orena and White (2015) found that children's evaluation of speaker knowledge influences their expectations towards the role of filled pauses in speech. Recently, Owens et al. (2018) presented opposite results, suggesting that children are not sensitive to the pauses, but rather to the semantics of the words, whereas the sensitivity to disfluencies develops later. The studies whose results have been reported above have defined disfluency in very different ways. Broen (1972: 10), for example, counted 'repeated or interjected sounds, words, or phrases' among the disfluencies while Kidd et al. (2011) considered only filled pauses. These are also addressed briefly in this chapter, but the central disfluency addressed are unfilled disfluency pauses, that is, hesitation pauses and self-interruptions as defined in Section 3.2.4. All disfluencies have been annotated following the CHAT conventions (MacWhinney 2009) on a separate tier in ELAN. The next section will illustrate the operationalisation of disfluency I developed for the present study with reference to a model proposed by Clark and Wasow (1998).

5.2 A model of disfluency pauses with reference to Qaqet

As already described in Section 3.2.4, in Qaqet, continuation marked intonation units, that usually show some kind of processing trouble, carry final level pitch, and the constituent before the pause is glottalised (Hellwig 2019: 140). During annotation it became clear that for both CDS and ADS, nearly all disfluency pauses occur with preposed function words, as shown in (38). This is true both for hesitation pauses and self-interruptions.

(38)   *tatrama.. amagama*
      ta=tat   ama   ama=gam-a   […]
      3PL.SBJ=take/pick_up   ART   ART=seed/fruit-DIST
      'they pick the.. the fruits […]' (PearARLA 079)

In example (38) the article *ama* is 'realized with level pitch and a final glottal stop as [amaP] […], signalling hesitation and the continuation of the utterance' (Hellwig 2019: 140). A pause follows, after which, in the case of hesitation pauses, the article is repeated, this time attached to the noun that is its lexical host. In the case of self-interruptions, of course, the utterance is abandoned after the pause. Clark and Wasow (1998) propose a four-step model for disfluency pauses that explains this process (see Table 5.1).

Instead of simply pausing when they have problems with a constituent, people who feel pressure to talk may choose to 'commit to a constituent by producing its first word or words […] as early as possible' (Clark & Wasow 1998: 235) (Stage I in Table 5.1).

Table 5.1: Four stages in repeating a word (table from Clark & Wasow 1998: 235), Qaqet examples added.

Stage	Speaker S's action	Spoken example from Qaqet
I. Initial commitment	S commits to a constituent	*ama* 'the'
II. Suspension of speech	S stops vocalising	{
III. Hiatus	S deals with potential delay	level pitch + final glottalisation
IV. Restart of constituent	S restarts the constituent, restoring continuity to it	} *amagataqi* 'the basket'

The insertion of function words before a hesitation pause can be explained by their low activation threshold (Levelt 1989: 203). Either the frequency or the predictability of a word is responsible for the low threshold. Clark and Wasow assume that people are 'pressed by a temporal imperative':

> If they delay too long, they may be heard as opting out, as confused or distracted, as uncertain about what they want to say, or as having nothing immediately to contribute. They can forestall these attributions by producing the first word of the next constituent (even if prematurely) to show that they are engaged in planning the constituent. (Clark & Wasow 1998: 238)

It is reasonable to assume that the experimental situation in the present study, telling the pear stories, made the participants feel a certain pressure to speak. They were in an unknown situation, being asked to retell a story and were even being recorded doing so. This may explain the large number of preposed function words uttered before hesitations found in the data. Still, impressionistically, this pattern also seems to prevail in the longitudinal recordings of our project (Hellwig personal communication).

Stage II in Table 5.1, the stop in vocalising, may be caused by various factors. At any level of speech planning, difficulties may arise so that the speaker needs additional processing time. These difficulties might include 'problems in segment retrieval or in implementing the articulation of the next syllable, replanning of the overall message or the grammatical structure, on-the-fly changes in lemma selection' (Himmelmann 2014: 950) or other factors that may cause the speakers to need more time. Clark and Wasow (1998) report broad evidence that speakers are more likely to suspend speaking the more complex the following constituent is (see also Kidd et al. 2011 for the relation between complicated, infrequent or discourse- new referents and hesitations).

Stage III in Table 5.1 is where a certain level of speaker agency may be relevant as Clark and Fox Tree (2002) report: speakers are able to anticipate the duration of an expected delay, and accordingly choose different means of dealing with it. In the Qaqet pear stories, speakers deal with the potential delay in speaking by holding level pitch and glottalising the constituent just before the pause, occasionally lengthening the last constituent.[1] This absence of hesitation particles in the pear story data supports a hypothesis formulated by Clark and Fox Tree (2002): that hesitation particles are not a 'symptom of trouble' but rather an interjection that comments on the actual performance of the speaker in announcing 'minor or major expected delays' in formulation (Clark & Fox Tree 2002: 79). As a symptom of processing trouble, it is to be expected that it can be found in all speakers of the world. As a linguistic sign, on the other hand, there may well be typological differences: in the languages described by Streeck (1996), lengthening is used as a hesitation sign, whereas in Qaqet, final level pitch and glottalisation are used (Hellwig 2019: 56).

Stage IV from Table 5.1, the repetition of the preposed function word, restores the continuity of the utterance. It is up until this step that self-interruptions and hesitations are identical. It is true for both that speakers need additional processing time and they handle their delay in some way, but in hesitations, they continue the previous intonation contour, and potentially try to restore its continuity, for example, by repeating the function word. Self-interruptions, conversely, are those disfluency pauses where the intonation contour is abandoned and, accordingly, no continuity has to be restored. Speakers can continue an intonation contour only until some 'upper limit' of time (Himmelmann 2014: 936), so the reset in intonation is rather a consequence of processing issues than of functional differences. This is why, for the following comparison of CDS and ADS in the next section, both phenomena are treated alike.

---

1   Himmelmann (2014: 942) reports for Tagalog (Philippines) and Streeck (1996: 208) for Ilokano (Philippines) and Lauje (Sulawesi, Indonesia) the lack of hesitation particles. Tagalog, Ilokano and Lauje all belong to the Malayo-Polynesian languages.

5.3 Disfluency pauses: Comparison of CDS and ADS

In this section, the two registers CDS and ADS will be compared in terms of disfluency pauses. For each speaker, two values have been calculated: disfluency pauses per 100 words in ADS and disfluency pauses per 100 words in CDS. The results are shown in Figure 5.1.

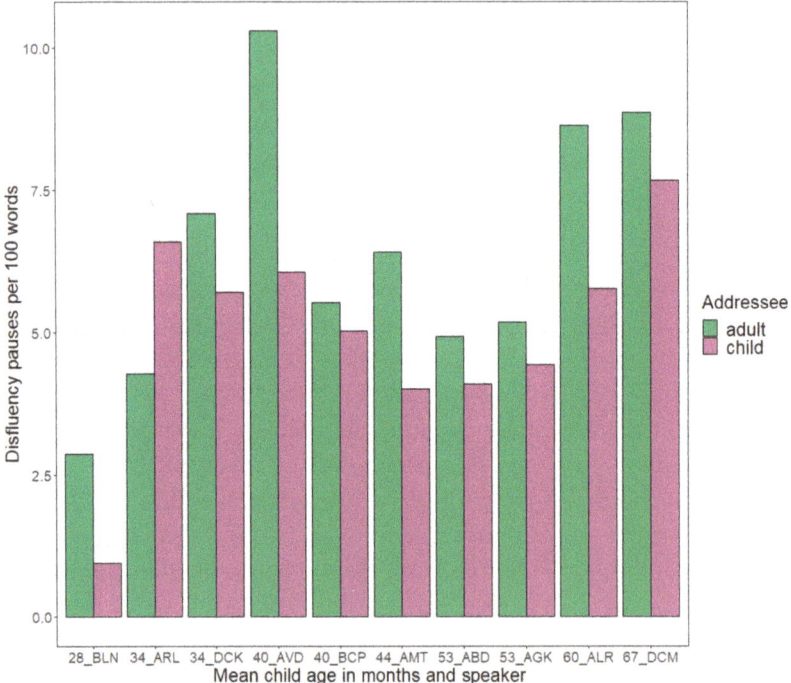

Figure 5.1: Disfluency pauses per 100 words ADS vs CDS.

Each pair of bars represents one speaker. The age of the child spoken to in months and its name code are given on the x-axis. On the y-axis, hesitations per 100 words are shown. All but one speaker is more fluent when speaking to a child. Only ARL hesitates more when talking to his son XAT (34m). The mean for ADS is 6.411 disfluency pauses per 100 words (SD = 2.316), and for CDS 5.033 disfluency pauses per 100 words (SD = 1.840). Due to the small size of the sample, a Wilcoxon-test for related samples was chosen. It yielded a significant difference in disfluency pauses per 100 words between ADS and CDS (Z = 48.000; p = 0.037).

This is consistent with previous research that describes a lower disfluency rate in CDS than in ADS. On the basis of these results, I expected that the proportion of disfluencies in CDS correlates with the age of the child, but a non-parametric Spearman test showed that this is not the case (r = 0.676, p = 0.152). There is therefore no clear connection between child age and CDS fluency. An explanation for these results is offered with reference to individual differences between speakers. These differences are large (see Figure 5.1). Speaker BLN was by far the most fluent speaker in CDS and in ADS, while speaker AVD hesitated a great deal in ADS and lay in the normal range for CDS. Furthermore, the hesitations were occasionally caused by the interactive style of the child. Out of the 28 times speaker DCK hesitated in the CDS-condition, 11 instances occurred when he saw his daughter ZEA look in another direction. At such times, he tried to get her attention by leaning over to her, calling her or tickling her shoulder. Similar evidence is reported by Nilsson Björkenstam et al. (2013) who find that many disfluencies are used as attention-directing signals.

For ARL, a closer examination of the interaction between the only adult speaker (a father) who hesitated more when talking to a child (XAT) helps to explain the results. XAT was the most interactive child in the pear story task, asking more questions than all the other children in the study (see example (39)).

(39) a. ARL: *iakamariaqiamabaketki*
        ia-ka=mat
        another-3SG.M.SBJ=take/pick_up
        ia-ki   ama=baket-ki
        another-NC.SG.F   ART=bucket-NC.SG.F
        'The other one takes another bucket…'
    b. XAT: *baketkiqua?*
        baket-ki   kua
        bucket-NC.SG.F   where/why
        'Where is the bucket?'
    c. ARL: *deqamuqi daa.. ilanyit braqi*
        de=ka=mu-ki   de=aa
        CONJ=3SG.M.SBJ=put-3SG.F loc.part=3sg.m.poss
        ilany-it   pet-ki
        foot/leg-NC.SG.LONG   on/under-NC.SG.F
        'and he puts it onto his.. bicycle'

d. XAT: *aailanyit braqiqua?*
aa=ilany-it
3SG.M.POSS=foot/leg-NC.SG.LONG
pet-ki   kua
on/under-3SG.F   where/why
'Where is his bicycle?'

e. ARL: *de.. iva de.. keuaisaqi*
de   ip-a   de   ke=uaik
CONJ   CONJ-DIST   CONJ   3SG.M.SBJ.NPST=run
se-ki
to/with-NC.SG.F
'and.. afterwards.. he leaves with it.' (PearARLP 065-070)

Instead of listening to the story, XAT often interrupted his father by asking for the location of things ARL mentioned during the story. ARL had to react constantly to the actions of his son and accordingly lost the thread of his narration. It is likely that this interactive style led to more hesitations, for example, in the case of (39e). The individual style of interaction between caregivers and children again plays a central role.

Still, for all speakers but one, CDS was more fluent than ADS. I next investigated whether the higher complexity of ADS causes its disfluency (see Section 5.1). I compared the MLU of all utterances with hesitations to the MLU of all utterances without hesitations.[2] The results for ADS are presented in Figure 5.2, and for CDS in Figure 5.3.

In ADS, the mean length of utterances with hesitations is 10.93 words (SD = 4.123), while utterances without hesitations have a mean length of 6.35 (SD = 3.620). For CDS, the corresponding values are 10.43 (SD = 3.707) words for utterances with hesitations and 5.18 (SD = 3.617) words for utterances without hesitations. This supports the hypothesis that utterance complexity in terms of utterance length is responsible for the higher rate of hesitations in ADS.

---

2   Note that self-interruptions are excluded from this count; only full intonation units are part of the calculation.

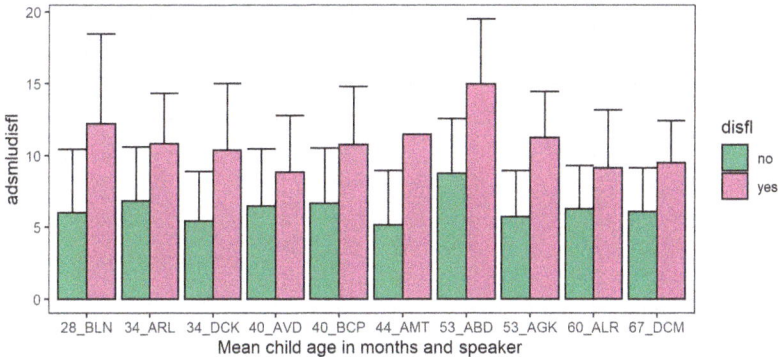

Figure 5.2: MLU of utterances with and without hesitations in ADS.

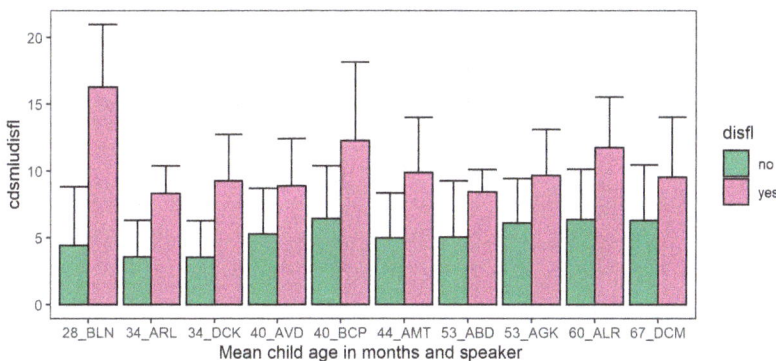

Figure 5.3: MLU of utterances with and without hesitations in CDS.

5.4 Distribution of hesitations

In Section 1.2 I explained that the location of a hesitation may tell a listener what to expect. To investigate this hypothesis, I annotated the stories (CDS and ADS) of those persons talking to the younger children (of 36 months or below) to determine the position of the hesitation: does it occur before a syntactic phrase boundary, in a situation in which the speaker has to plan what to say next or before a new referent is introduced?[3] For self-interruptions, it is difficult to judge whether the constituent after the pause is what makes people hesitate. As the original

---

3 Previous studies reporting hesitations at potentially helpful positions (Kidd et al. 2011) have child participants up to three years of age, so I excluded the data from the older children.

utterance is abandoned, the constituent after the pause is not necessarily uttered. Accordingly, only hesitation pauses have been included in the following analysis.

As a matter of fact, in the pear stories, the speakers hesitate often because they are trying to remember what happened in the film. This is typically what happens at the beginning of the stories (see example (40)). ARL has just started to tell the pear story to his friend ACP, but has not yet figured out how to start his story.

(40) *amasiitka de tikai..*
ama=siit-ka   de   tika=i
ART=story-NC.SG.M   CONJ   EMPH=CONJ
'the story, so..' (PearARLA 001)
iak deqatikaqe..
ia-ka   de=ka=tika=ke
another-NC.SG.M   CONJ=3SG.M.SBJ=EMPH=3SG.M.SBJ.NPST
'a man, he..' (PearARLA 002)

Example (40) seems to be a typical instance of what Chafe calls 'finding the focus of consciousness'. He distinguishes this from a second reason to hesitate:

> the speaker's need to find the next focus. Others, as we will see at the end of this discussion, stem from the need to find the best way to verbalize a focus, once found. In other words, sometimes speakers hesitate while they are deciding *what* to talk about next, and sometimes they hesitate while they are deciding *how* to talk about what they have chosen. (Chafe 1985: 171)

For some people from Raunsepna, there are a considerable number of unusual referents in the pear film. There are no goats in Raunsepna, nor pears or bicycles (children have probably never seen one). The goat especially receives many labels (from 'thingy' to 'cow', 'horse', 'dog' and 'donkey') and people hesitate frequently before referring to it (see (41)).

Here, ABD first does not know how to describe the sound the man hears ('He hears the sound of.. well some thingy'), then she explicitly comments that she recalled the word ('They call it goat'). In the following description, she still hesitates before uttering the word *goatkia*. She obviously knows what she wants to talk about, but is searching for the right word to express her thoughts.

(41) a. ABD: *kanarli samerama.. kerl amamaqia*
ka=narli se=met=ama
3SG.M.SBJ=hear/feel to/with=in=ART
kerl ama=ma-ki-a
DEONT ART=thingy-NC.SG.F-DIST
'He hears the sound of.. well of some thingy'
b. ABD: *iratiski amagoatki [...]*
i=ta=tis-ki
CONJ=3PL.SBJ=callsay-NC.SG.F
ama=goat-ki
ART=goat-NC.SG.F
'They call it goat [...]'
c. ABD: *kiqerl iakekiurlet meraa.. aagoatkia*
kiqerl ia-ka=kiurlet
EMPH another-NC.SG.M=pull
met=aa aa=goat-ki-a
in=3SG.M.POSS 3SG.M.POSS=goat-NC.SG.F-DIST
'A man pulls his.. his goat' (PearABDA 035-038)

In Section 5.1 I reported previous research that found hesitations to be predictive of unknown or difficult referents and phrase boundaries, especially in CDS. Example (41) is one instance of such a situation. Other hesitations precede clausal and phrasal boundaries, see (42). Those might help children identify syntactic structures.

(42) *sagel luqia draawilwilki ip.. ip kirlguirl*
se=gel lu-ki-a
to/with=close DEM-NC.SG.F-DIST
de=araa=wilwil-ki ip
LOC.PART=3PL.POSS=bicycle-NC.SG.F CONJ
ip ki=rlguirl
CONJ 3SG.F.SBJ.NPST=return
'[the man whistles] to the woman on her bicycle so that.. so that she will come back' (PearABDP 091)

Occasionally, a hesitation is influenced by lexical choice (see (43)). BLN hesitates when she wants to refer to the goat and calls it *danggi* 'dog' instead of *goatki* or, the term she uses when talking to her husband, *amamaqi taquarl amahoski* 'Something like a horse'. During transcription of the relevant example, BLN commented that she decided to talk about an animal she knows her son, ZDL (28), is familiar with. So in this case, the adaptation of the input to the child interlocutor produced a hesitation pause, allowing BLN to select the appropriate referent.

(43)   […] *katden kanaa.. aadanggi*
       ka=tden   ka=ne=aa
       3SG.M.SBJ=come   3SG.M.SBJ=from/with=3SG.M.POSS
       aa=dang-ki
       3SG.M.POSS=dog-NC.SG.F
       '… He comes with his.. his dog' (PearBLNP 031)

5.5 Summary: Disfluencies in Qaqet CDS

In this chapter, I compared the number of disfluency pauses (both self-interruptions and hesitation pauses) in ADS and CDS. Nearly all of the hesitation pauses involve a function word uttered before the pause. There are significantly more disfluency pauses in ADS than in CDS, both for fathers' and mothers' speech, but the difference does not correlate with child age. These results confirm previous research proposing a high degree of fluency as typical for CDS. The difference in length between utterances with and without MLU indicates that the lower complexity of CDS is responsible for its fluency.

Additionally, the results show that fluency (at least with reference to hesitations) is not directly related to comprehensibility. Both in CDS and ADS, uncommon referents provoke hesitations. Kidd et al. (2011) found that even small children are sensitive to hesitations announcing complicated referents. There are also hesitations at phrase boundaries, possibly enabling the listeners to locate those boundaries.

Several hesitations in the data are related to the interaction between adult speakers and child listeners. Hesitations are often provoked, for example, because children do not listen and the speakers interrupt themselves to get their attention back, or a child is too interactive and the speaker, busy responding to his or her questions, hesitates as he tries to find his way back to the story. Sometimes, the linguistic adjustments used to adapt speech to children's needs provoke hesitations. Speakers may need additional planning time for the relevant adjustments.

The evidence presented in this chapter suggests that the effects of interaction are more relevant than age for fluency in CDS. This factor could be controlled for by excluding those disfluencies that are caused by interactional features. Still, disfluencies are potentially helpful as cues for referential intentions and identification of salient structures. This has also been proposed for the typical prosodic features of CDS, which are the topic of the next chapter.

6
Prosodic features

6.1 Previous research on prosodic features of CDS

In many languages, the mean fundamental frequency of adults' speech is higher when they talk to young children, and adults also use a wider frequency range than in ADS. This has been documented for English (Remick 1976; Garnica 1977), German (Fernald & Simon 1984), French, Italian, German, Japanese, British and American English (Fernald et al. 1989), and for the tonal language Mandarin (Grieser & Kuhl 1988). All of these studies use semi-spontaneous data, manipulating the addressee variable but otherwise trying to hold the situation as natural as possible. Only Garnica (1977) uses elicited production data from various language games.

Previous research has shown that the prosodic features typical for CDS figure most prominently in speech to children up to one year of age (Saxton 2015). Hence, researchers occasionally refer to infant-directed speech (IDS) as a separate register from CDS. However, the typical adaptations have also been attested in speech to older children. Ratner and Pye (1984) show that the speech of US-American mothers speaking English to children of 32.5 months has a significantly higher pitch than when talking to adults. Garnica (1977) reports the same for children of 27 months. However, the speech to children of 65 months did not show a significantly higher fundamental frequency than speech to adults. Yet, the frequency range was significantly higher than ADS for both age groups. Warren-Leubecker and Bohannon (1984) found that mothers had a higher fundamental frequency both when talking to children of 24 and of 60 months of age. Although Warren-Leubecker and Bohannon referred to Garnica's study, they did not comment on the differences found for mothers' speech to the older children.

The fathers in the study by Warren-Leubecker and Bohannon (1984), as opposed to the mothers, hardly altered their fundamental frequency when talking to the 60-month-olds, although they did so when talking to 24-month-olds. These reports show that both the sex of the person talking to the child, and the child's age, are variables that have to be taken into account.

For speaking rate, it has been reliably documented that CDS is slower when adults address infants (Broen 1972). Fernald et al. (1989) report longer pauses in infant-directed speech in their cross-linguistic study, a feature Goldman-Eisler (1973) has shown to be responsible for the lower speaking rate in CDS. Such adaptations give the listener more time for processing, which might support comprehension. Given this ample evidence, prosodic modifications have been hypothesised to be a universal feature of CDS (Sachs 1977).

However, few studies have addressed non-WEIRD societies (see Section 1.1 and Section 1.2). The studies that do exist do not always confirm the predictions. At least two studies report diverging evidence: in K'iche' Maya, adults occasionally even use a lower pitch when they address children of 25.3 months (Ratner & Pye 1984). K'iche' mothers' speaking rate does not differ from ADS either, or is even slightly increased (Pye 1986b). Conversely, there are other studies on non-WEIRD societies that do confirm the predictions from Western, urban societies. Broesch and Bryant (2014), using semi-spontaneous data, report for Kenyan, Fijian and North American mothers that all used a higher pitch, a greater pitch variation and fewer syllables per second. Those features have been suggested to foster attention, emotional bonding and identification of boundaries (Fernald 1992; Broesch & Bryant 2014). Golinkoff et al. (2015: 340) propose that 'exaggerated intonational characteristics highlight the structural properties of utterances, and provide information about how speech "chunks" together'. The distribution of those characteristics within utterances is then of central importance. Fernald (1992) found that English mothers place words denoting new referents utterance-finally and mark them with an exaggerated intonation when talking to infants. They hypothesised that 'adults may also be biased to provide relevant linguistic information at positions of perceptual prominence in the speech stream'

(Fernald 1992: 209). Children also give special attention to utterance ends (Weisleder & Waxman 2010). The information presented utterance-finally therefore has a special status.

One of the typologically unusual features of Qaqet is that intonation units (IUs) tend to have a flat contour, with all major pitch movements taking place at their right boundary (Hellwig 2019: 56). Do these prosodic characteristics also hold for CDS or are they more evenly distributed across the intonation unit? In the first case, they may be helpful only for identifying borders of whole intonation units, and not for identifying smaller units. While I will not deal with this question systematically in the present study, I will offer preliminary insights from the corpus. To summarise, much research on non-Western, rural societies confirms the pattern found for WEIRD languages, but there are counter-examples like K'iche' or Pitjantjatjara. Given the evidence reported above, and speakers' reports (see Section 2.2.4) that adults, especially mothers, adapt their speech to children, I hypothesise that CDS in Qaqet shows the typical prosodic features, that is, a higher frequency range and a higher mean fundamental frequency. Likewise, a slow speech rate is to be expected in the data, especially given that adults in Raunsepna confirm that this feature is typical and useful for communication with small children. As for the mean length of utterance (Chapter 4), I found a turning point in the data that appeared in speech to children at around 40 months, so I expect to find a similar turning point for prosodic features.

6.2 Method and results

6.2.1 Frequency

The recordings were not made with head-mounted microphones as is recommended for studies in phonology (Klimes 2017), but with the internal microphone of the Zoom Q8 (see Section 3.1.2). While a head-mounted microphone only records the voice of a participant, a microphone placed in the room is susceptible to acoustic interferences. Nevertheless, all data were checked for audio quality, and intonation units with major interference were excluded. The data from speaker BLN had to be excluded entirely from the analysis: in the ADS-session, there is constant overlap from a crying child. Once I had deleted those units with interference from other voices, there were not enough segments left for analysis.

For each intonation unit, F_0, F_{max} and F_{min} were extracted using Praat software (Boersma & Weenink 2021). Then a mean was calculated for each speaker in semitones for the sake of comparability. Calculating in semitones makes the data easier to interpret as they correspond to the musical scales. An interval of one semitone is clearly distinguishable for the human ear. The total frequency range was obtained by subtracting the mean F_{min} from the mean F_{max}. The frequency range analysed was 75–300Hz, all the values are provided in semitones (st, reference value 100 Hz).

The results for the frequency extraction are given in Table 6.1.

Table 6.1: Mean F0 (ADSm,CDSm), total F0 range (ADSr,CDSr), difference between ADS and CDS for mean F0 (MeanDiff) and difference between ADS and CDS for total F0 range (RaDi).

Age, ID	ADSm	CDSm	ADSr	CDSr	MeanDiff	RaDi
34, DCK	81.20	83.03	5.00	6.82	1.84	1.83
34, ARL	85.76	89.68	6.90	8.89	3.92	1.99
40, AVD	81.56	81.98	3.96	7.40	0.42	3.44
40, BCP	82.45	84.90	8.20	8.87	2.45	0.67
44, AMT	91.50	92.57	9.93	11.29	1.07	1.36
53, ABD	91.90	93.32	8.86	11.41	1.42	2.55
53, AGK	90.70	91.39	7.47	8.48	0.69	1.01
60, ALR	93.20	91.65	7.14	11.77	-1.55	4.63
67, DCM	81.27	81.84	5.14	10.42	0.56	5.28

The mean difference in fundamental frequency between ADS and CDS is 1.20 st (SD = 1.51), for frequency range it is 2.53 st (SD = 1.61). A Wilcoxon-test showed that the difference between CDS and ADS for mean F_0 is not significant (Z = 6.0; p = 0.051). For the total frequency range, the test showed that they differ significantly (Z = 45.0; p = 0.008). The results are illustrated in Figure 6.1 and Figure 6.2.

The difference in mean pitch (r = −0.672; p = 0.047) furthermore correlates negatively with the age of the child listeners, see Figure 6.3. As for MLU (Chapter 4), there is a turning point, at around 40 months, where the difference between ADS and CDS decreases.

6. PROSODIC FEATURES

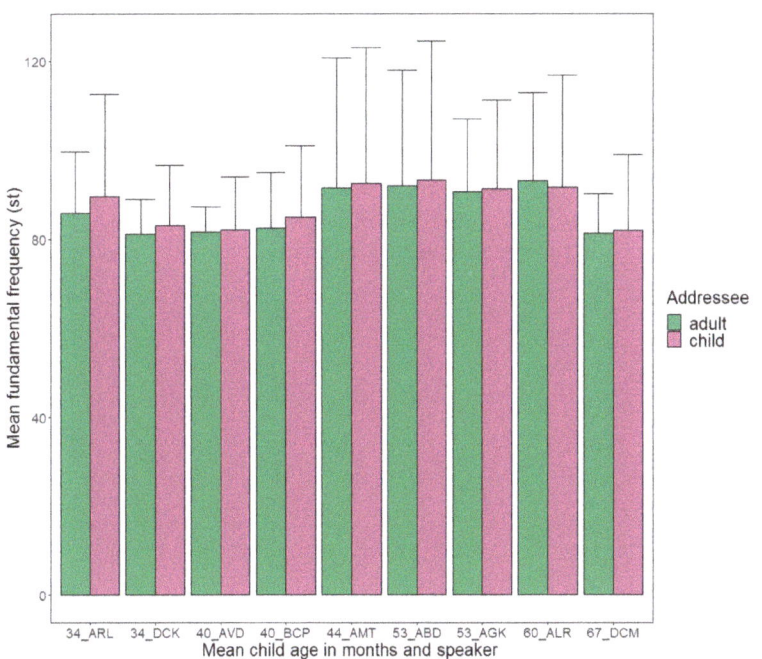

Figure 6.1: Mean fundamental frequency for ADS and CDS.

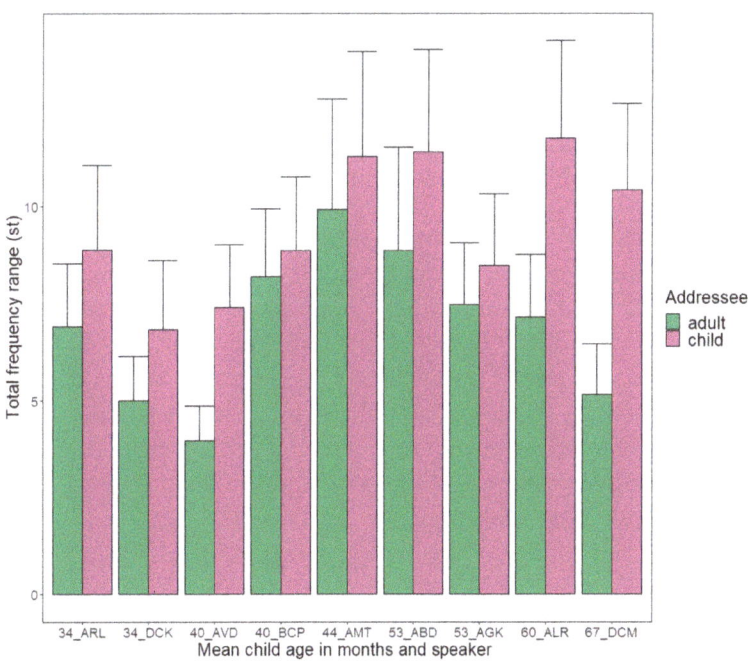

Figure 6.2: Total frequency range for ADS and CDS.

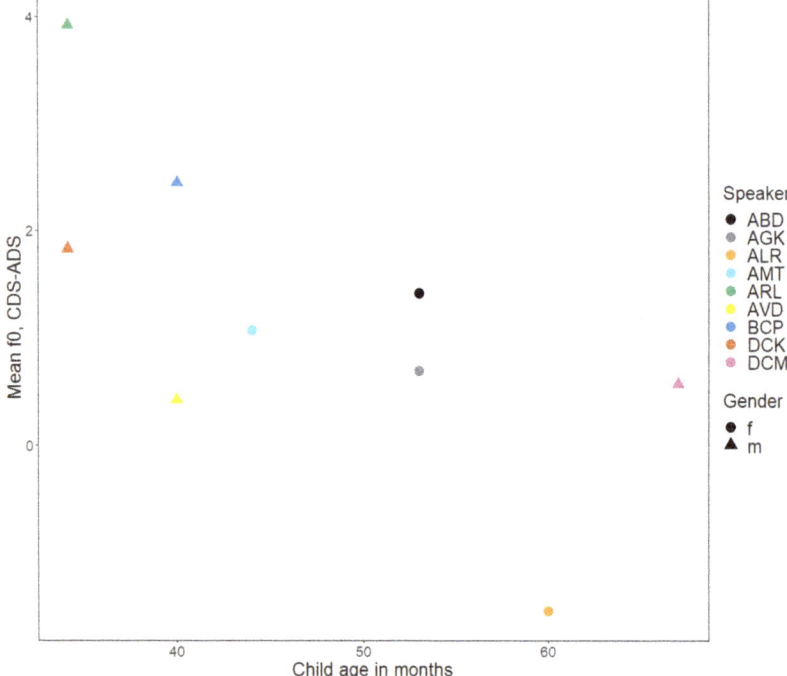

Figure 6.3: Difference between CDS and ADS for mean fundamental frequency.

Yet, the difference in pitch range does not diminish as the children mature (Spearman; r = 0.487; p = 0.183). On the contrary, at the upper age range of the child participants, the frequency ranges are even higher than for the younger children (ALR, DCM), see Figure 6.4.

This suggests that the turning point for the frequency range is later than the turning point for a higher mean fundamental frequency, as reported by Garnica (1977). In order to explore those pitch movements further, the following section briefly examines their location within IUs in Qaqet CDS in comparison to ADS. The highest pitch movements in Qaqet ADS are located IU-finally (Hellwig 2019). In order to investigate the pitch movements, I chose examples with largely similar content from CDS and ADS for two female speakers and one male speaker, and extracted their intonation contours (see Section 3.2.3).

6. PROSODIC FEATURES

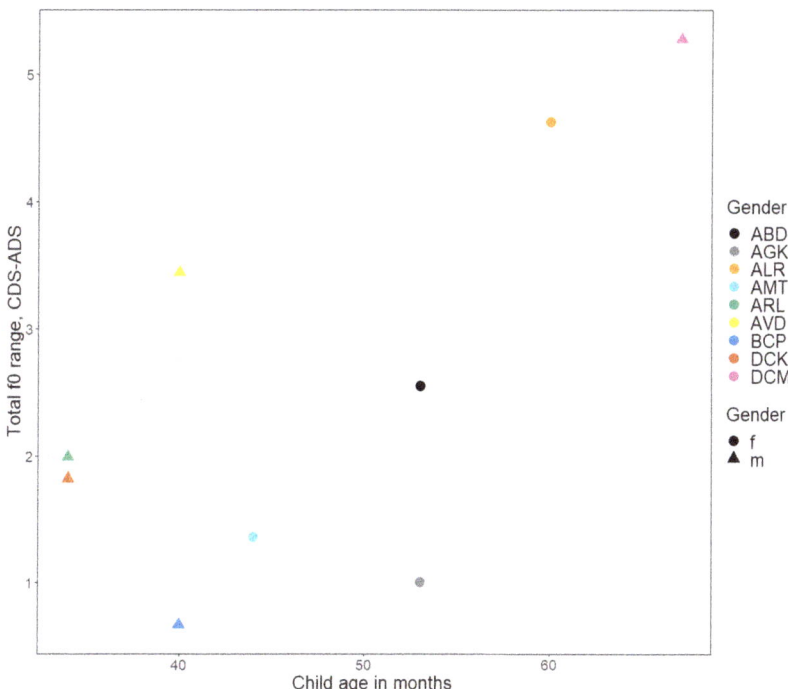

Figure 6.4: Difference between CDS and ADS for total frequency range.

Both in Figure 6.5 (44, CDS) and Figure 6.6 (45, ADS), there is a final rise-fall (CDS 3.3 st rise and 1 st fall; ADS 5.3 st rise and 1.2 st fall), and also a general downdrift in the utterances before the rise (CDS 3.9 st; ADS 2.9 st).

The steepest movements are likewise located at the end of the units.

(44) *qeqiuaiqiamanu*
 ke=qiuaik i-a-manu
 3SG.M.SBJ.NPST=run away-DIR-across
 'He goes away' (PearBCPP 67)

(45) *qui qatden saqianamuk*
 kui ka=tden se-ki
 quoting 3SG.M.SBJ=come to/with-3SG.F
 a-na-muk
 DIR-back-across
 'He comes with the things' (PearBCPA 030)

113

For ALR, both CDS (Figure 6.9, 46) and ADS (Figure 6.8, 47) show a general downdrift of 3st and a final fall (CDS 5.4 st; ADS 2st).

(46) *beiva deqatit*
      de=ip-a   de=ka=tit
      CONJ=PURP-DIST   CONJ=3SG.M.SBJ=go
      'And he goes' (PearALRP 029)

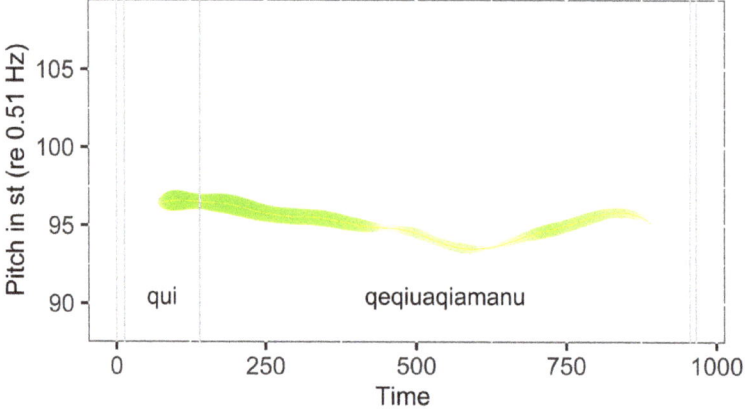

Figure 6.5: Intonation contour for CDS (44), male speaker.

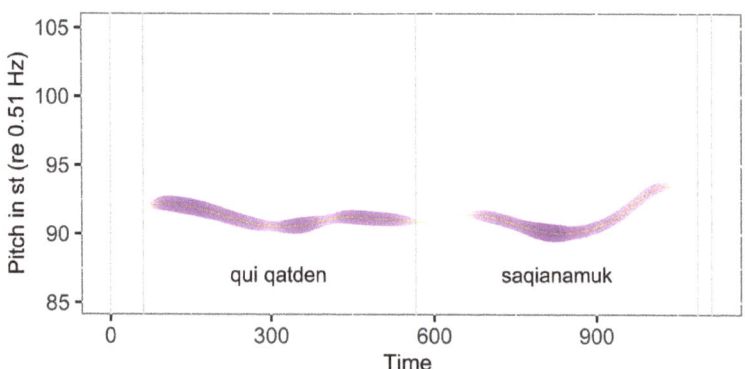

Figure 6.6: Intonation contour for ADS (45), male speaker.

(47) *luqa deqatit*
      de=ka=tika   lu-k-a
      CONJ=3SG.M.SBJ=EMPH   DEM-NC.3G.M-DIST
      de=ka=tit
      CONJ=3SG.M.SBJ=go
      'And this man too he goes' (PearALRA 137)

The pattern repeats for the last speaker, AGK, for both CDS (Figure 6.9, 48) and ADS (Figure 6.10, 49). There are no major movements within the unit, but there is a rise of 7.5st followed by a fall of 6.7st in CDS and equally a rise of 9st followed by a fall of 4st in ADS, both in utterance final position.

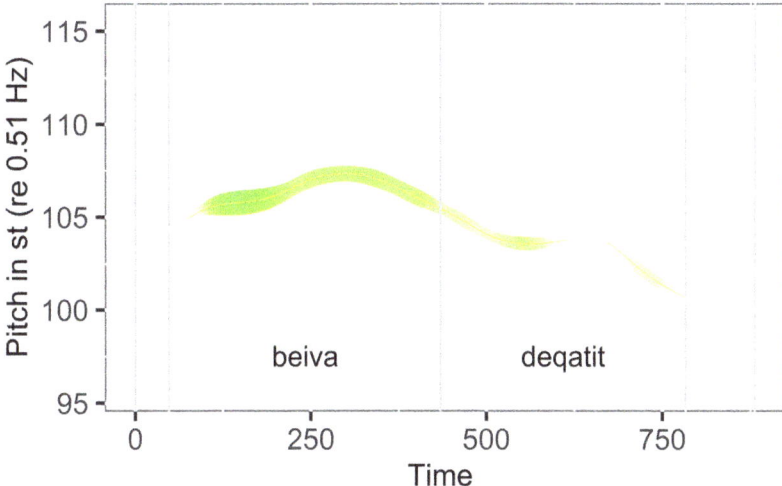

Figure 6.7: Intonation contour for CDS(46), female speaker.

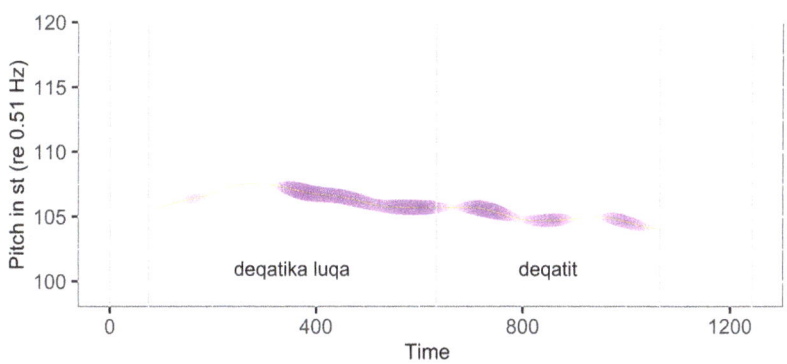

Figure 6.8: Intonation contour for ADS (47), female speaker.

(48)   *amangerlmamga qatirinamuk*
       ama=ngerlmam-ka   ka=tit-i=ne=muk
       ART=man/father-NC.SG.M   3SG.M.SBJ=go-SIM=from/with=across
       'Another man comes' (PearAGKP 028)

(49) *luqa amangerlmamga qatirimanep*
    lu-ka-a   ama=ngerlmam-ka
    DEM-NC.SG.M-DIST   ART=man/father-NC.SG.M
    ka=tit-i-manep
    3SG.M.SBJ=go-SIM-down
    'This man goes down' (PearAGKA 051)

Based on these primary insights, the hypothesis would be that the distribution of pitch contours in CDS mirrors the patterns found in ADS. The exaggerated pitch movements at the end of intonation could make it easier for children to identify the boundaries of intonation units, but not to identify boundaries within intonation units (e.g. at the word-level). This is further supported by the habit several children displayed when listening to the stories. They repeated the end of the previous adult utterances with the intonation of a polar question (see (50)). ZDL repeats the last part of his mother BLN's utterance two times, both times with the intonation of a polar question. BLN confirms both times.

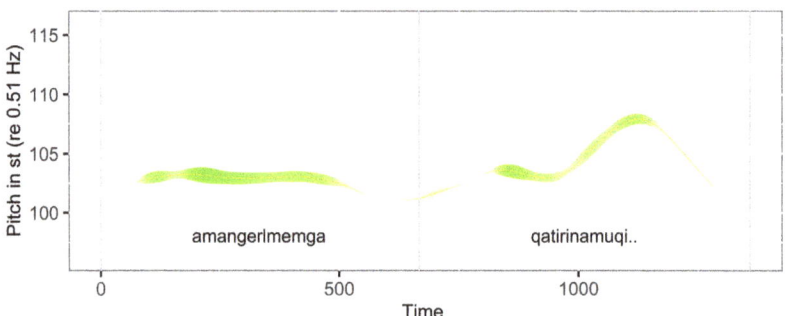

Figure 6.9: Intonation contour for CDS (48), female speaker.

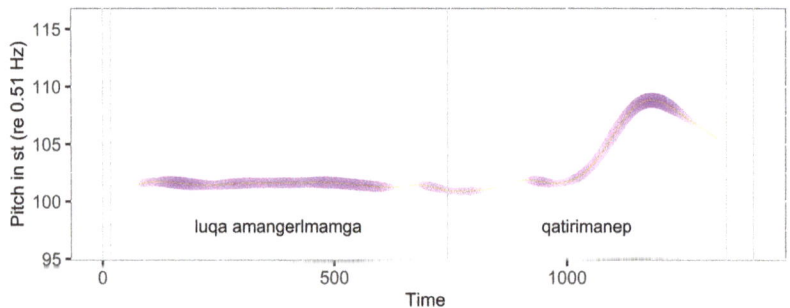

Figure 6.10: Intonation contour for ADS (48), female speaker.

(50) a. BLN: *iqeqiuaik daacarki*
i=ke=qiuaik
SIM=3SG.M.SBJ.NPST=run
de=aa=car-ki
LOC.PART=3SG.M.POSS=car-NC.SG.F
'And he runs by car.'
b. ZDL: *karki?*
kar-ki
car-nc.sg.f
'Car?'
b. BLN: *ee. amagilki*
ee ama=gil-ki
yes ART=small-NC.SG.F
'Yes, a small one.'
c. ZDL: *gilki?*
gil-ki
NM=small-NC.SG.F
'A small one?'
d. BLN: *mm* mm
yes
'Yes' (PearBLNP 54-60)

ZDL shows that his special attention is directed towards the part of the utterance that is marked by pitch movements. He echoes *gilki*, echoing his mothers' utterance incompletely. While providing feedback that he is attending to what his mother says, his utterance works equally as a clarification request that is confirmed by BLN *mm*.

A similar routine is described for children in Trackton, U.S. by Heath (2009):

> Here they seem to be remembering fragments of speech and repeating these without any active production. (Heath 2009: 91)

Heath described several 'stages of participation' Trackton children experience during their second year of life. The first stage is marked by complete imitation, followed by a stage that adds some variation to the theme. In the last stage, they fully enter the conversation. The first stage seems to be very similar to the Qaqet technique, but there is a slight difference. While Trackton children initially merely echoed what they heard, including the original intonation, the Qaqet children changed it into a polar question, which adults then confirm.

In this section, I have presented evidence that ADS and CDS in Qaqet differ in their intonation patterns, that the ends of utterances are prosodically prominent in Qaqet and that children also preferably attend to them. In Section 6.2.2, I compare the speaking rate of Qaqet ADS and CDS.

6.2.2 Speaking rate

The speaking rate was calculated by dividing the total number of words by the total duration of all intonation units of a single speaker, thereby obtaining words per second. The difference in speaking rate between ADS (m = 4.6; SD = 0.6) and CDS (m = 4.6; SD = 0.4), as revealed by a nonparametric Wilcoxon-test for related samples, is not significant (Z = 24.0; p = 0.721). Adults do not talk significantly slower to children than to adults. The individual results for each speaker are illustrated in Figure 6.11.

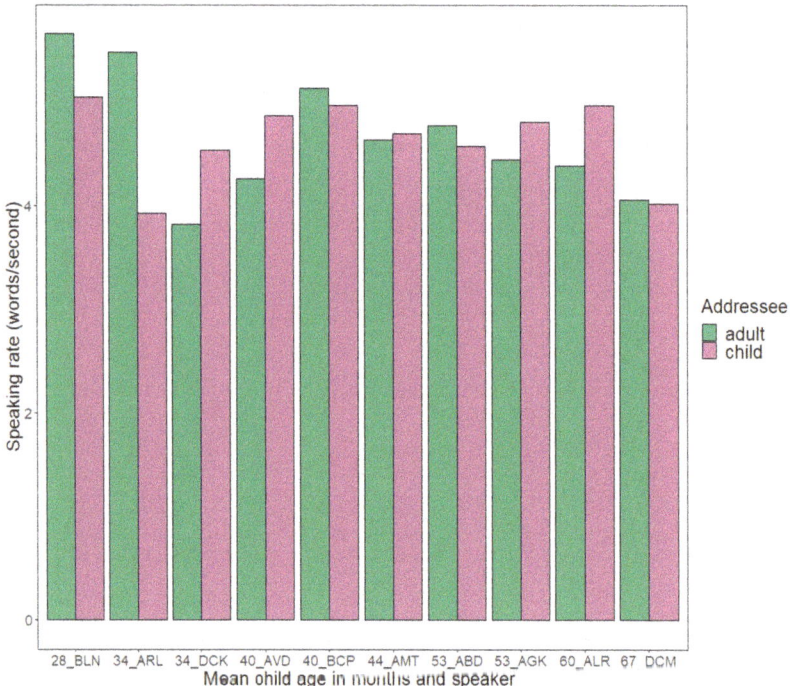

Figure 6.11: Speaking rate in words per second ADS vs CDS.

6. PROSODIC FEATURES

From Figure 6.11 we note that for the two speakers, BLN and ARL alone, the speaking rate is markedly lower in CDS than in ADS. Table 6.2 shows that the results obtained for Qaqet are totally different from the rates reported by Broen (1972). Broen recorded 132 words per minute in ADS, while in Qaqet I recorded 280.2. For CDS, the numbers also differ: while there are 278.7 words per minute in Qaqet, Broen recorded 115 words per minute.

Table 6.2: Words per minute CDS and ADS in comparison with results from Broen (1972).

Language	ADS	CDS
English	132	115
Qaqet	280.2	278.7

This considerable difference is partly caused by my methodological decision to count clitics as full words. Furthermore, the exclusion of inter-IU pauses in the Qaqet count has to be considered. Goldman-Eisler (1973) found that speaking rate depends on time spent pausing, not on time spent articulating. This might also explain the missing difference between CDS and ADS in the present study. O'Grady (2005) reported for English that the pauses in CDS were longer than in ADS. My testing procedure, excluding those pauses, thus may have failed to measure the desired variable. Accordingly, I measured the mean pause length for each speaker in CDS and ADS, respectively. I analysed only pauses between two IUs by the same speaker. The results are displayed in Table 6.3 and Figure 6.12.

Table 6.3: Mean pause length (ms) ADS and CDS, standard deviation (SD) and difference between ADS and CDS (diff).

Age, ID	ADS Mean	ADS SD	CDS Mean	CDS SD	diff
28, BLN	567.51	577.504	495.95	500.936	−71.56
34, ARL	846.16	650.690	545.68	430.094	−300.49
34, DCK	715.32	626.995	977.65	587.228	262.33
40, AVD	1,149.54	755.115	920.71	579.162	−228.82
40, BCP	786.70	667.048	803.67	661.535	16.97
44, AMT	596.79	697.551	643.97	439.862	47.18
53, ABD	837.59	672.605	851.09	645.334	13.50
53, AGK	676.50	639.208	739.43	723.681	62.92
60, ALR	679.84	723.056	792.06	674.915	112.23
67, DCM	1,163.60	882.361	1,019.23	780.095	−144.37

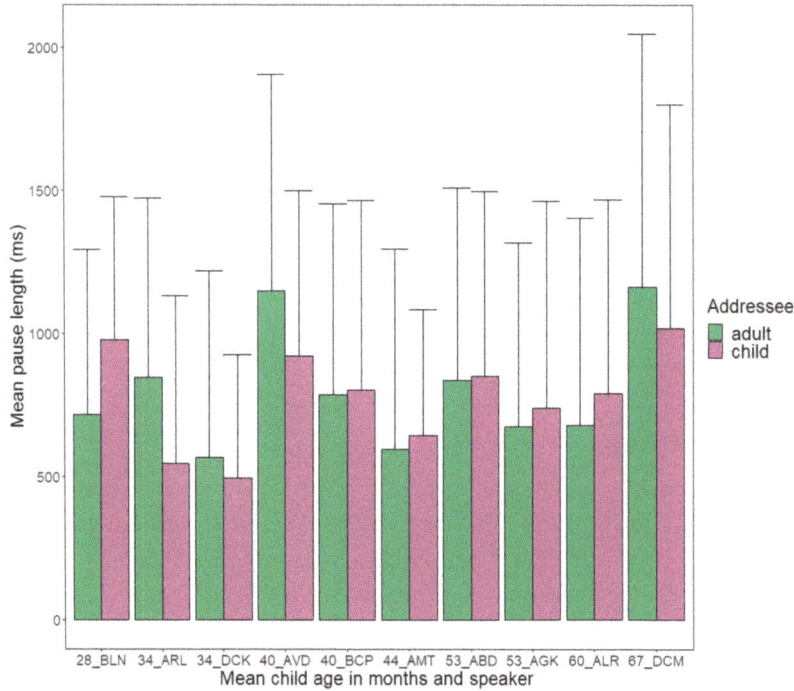

Figure 6.12: Pause length CDS vs ADS.

A Wilcoxon-test confirmed that CDS does not differ significantly from ADS in pause length (Z = 25.0; p = 0.799). Neither does the difference in pause length between ADS and CDS correlate with child age (Spearman coefficient: r = 0.079; p = 0.828). From Figure 6.12, I noticed that the (comparably) shorter pause lengths seem to be found in the stories directed at the talkative children. I therefore tested if there was a correlation between CDS pause length and the number of child utterances, but did not find one (Z = 0.644; p = 0.061).

6.3 Summary: Prosodic features of CDS in Qaqet

To summarise, speaking rate does not differ between CDS and ADS but is exceptionally high when compared to previous results (Broen 1972). Impressionistically, the pace of speech in both CDS and ADS is quite high. However, both the mean fundamental frequency (with near-significance) and the total frequency range differ between CDS and ADS in Qaqet. The mean fundamental frequency is furthermore negatively correlated with child age: the biggest differences between ADS and CDS are found in speech to children of up to 40 months of age. For all of the older children, the difference is around one semitone.

While the mean fundamental frequency difference decreases with increasing child age, the highest frequency ranges are found in speech towards the oldest children. This is consistent with findings from Garnica (1977). She found that the increased frequency range persisted longer in speech towards children than the increased mean pitch. With regard to their function, it seems likely that the pitch modifications serve to attract the children's attention. This is a necessary condition to fulfill common communicative goals (Broesch & Bryant 2014). Additionally, the modifications may signal positive emotional affect (Fernald & Mazzie 1991).

Preliminary results indicate that the largest pitch movements are located utterance-finally in both CDS and ADS. The attested intonation contours in Qaqet serve different communicative functions (Hellwig 2019). In the above discussion, I have presented contours that signal non-final and final units of declarative utterances. These are, by nature, connected to the organisation of turns. The indicators of these functions are promoted into a more salient position by exaggerating their frequency range. The communicative function is therefore also salient in children's perception. This is indicated by evidence that Qaqet children repeat the ends of utterances. Possibly, then, the attested differences could be helpful in the acquisition of turn-taking practices by directing the listeners' attention to the relevant modifications. Attracting and directing children's attention will again be a salient topic in Chapter 7 on speech acts.

7

Directing attention: Speech acts in Qaqet CDS-narratives

7.1 Previous research on speech acts in CDS

Previous research comparing ADS and CDS in several languages has repeatedly shown the presence of more directives and questions in CDS than in ADS. Broen (1972) reported an average of 23.4 per cent of mothers' utterances to be imperatives as they speak to young children and an average of 37 per cent to be questions. In Newport et al. (1977) 18 per cent of the utterances directed to children consisted of directives. In his study comparing CDS and ADS data for K'iche' Maya, Pye (1986a) found a marked increase of imperatives in CDS, ranging from 50 to 79 per cent in the CDS-data compared to 0–5 per cent in the ADS-data, whereas there were more questions in ADS than in CDS. Defina (2020) also reports a high number of imperatives in her exploration of Pitjantjatjara CDS.

For questions, Remick (1976) reported rates of 26–57 per cent in CDS, while they were nearly absent in ADS. Newport et al. (1977) and Snow (1977b) also found significantly more questions in CDS than in ADS. Cross (1977) demonstrated that the proportion of questions in mothers' speech declines as the child matures.

Thus, all previous studies report that CDS contains more directives. Only in K'iche' are they reported to be less frequent in CDS than in ADS. Vogt et al. (2015) offer an explanation for this by providing evidence that different speech styles are connected to different community types. A directive style with a marked increase of imperatives is found in typical non-Western, rural societies associated with communal action autonomy as a socialisation principle. A high volume of questions, on the other hand, is a sign of a large number of cognitive intentions expressed in language, and related to Western, urban societies where individual psychological autonomy is the driving principle. Based on this evidence, for the current study I expect a marked increase of imperatives in CDS compared to ADS. I expect the rate of questions in CDS to be in negative correlation with the age of the addressed child. It could be argued that I constructed a scenario rather typical of WEIRD societies by carrying out the pear story experiment. Therefore, it is to be expected that there will accordingly be many questions in CDS, as the activity type itself emphasises cognitive intentions.

In the CDS-data, most of the utterances described in the following serve the attention-directing function. Child-directed speech has been found to contain more attentionals than adult-directed speech (Shatz & Gelman 1973). Shatz and Gelman explain this by the lower attentional capacities of children, which provoke adults to continuously try to catch the children's attention. Gallaway and Richards (1994: 263) state that 'focusing the child's attention on the interaction [...] *and* on relevant aspects of the context is a necessary condition for the acquisition of a language and for successful communication'. Content questions, for instance, serve to direct the children's attention to the relevant aspects of the conversation. They elicit speech, and thereby enable conversational participation. Both of these functions are considered facilitating factors in CDS (Richards & Gallaway 1994: 264). In the present chapter, I will describe the interaction between adults and children in terms of communicative functions. The very first step was to decide on an appropriate coding system, which I describe in Section 7.2.

7.2 Data coding and selection

For the coding of speech acts, I used the INCA-A (Inventory of Communicative Acts – Abridged) by Ninio et al. (1994) as a basis, as recommended by MacWhinney (2000) for the analysis with CLAN-tools that are designed specifically for the quantitative analysis of child language. Ninio et al. (1994) propose the annotation of two levels of interaction, the illocutionary force type on the utterance-level, and the interchange type, which categorises a sequence of interactions. For the current data, I have only annotated the illocutionary force type because it sufficiently differentiates the speech acts in question. The identification of a speaker's intention, which is necessary for the categorisation of a speech act (Ninio et al. 1994: 169), is not a straightforward matter. Here, I used a combination of syntactic, prosodic, semantic and pragmatic features to identify the different speech acts.

Only those types of speech acts that serve to organise the interaction between speakers are addressed. This applies to questions, imperatives and some additional utterances like vocatives and interjections. Chafe offers a terminology for the subdivision of different types of intonation units:

> The successful units can be subcategorized into those that convey substantive ideas of events, states, or referents and those that have regulatory functions in the sense of regulating interaction or information flow. (Chafe 1994: 63)

The substantive units in the data are identified by speakers' illocution. This is restricted to informing the listener of what happened in the film. During annotation, they received a separate code, and were excluded from further analysis. The regulatory units are the focus of the current chapter. An utterance like (51) was categorised as substantive, as the speaker was only talking about what she had seen in the film. An utterance like (52) is a regulatory intonation unit because the speaker has intentions other than providing information about what she saw in the film, namely, eliciting information from the listener.

(51) *katramagama*
      ka=tat   ama=gam-a
      3SG.M.SBJ=take/pick_up   ART=seed/fruit-DIST
      'He picks fruits' (PearABDP 033)

(52) *nadamagiqi?*
ne=de=ama=gi-ki
from/with=LOC.PART=ART=what-NC.SG.F
'Where from?' (PearABDP 024)

Both the individual differences and the differences between ADS and CDS in the amount of regulatory or substantive IUs are quite high, as seen in Table 7.1.

For some people, like AGK, ALR and AVD, there is a low degree of variation between CDS and ADS and they have high levels of substantive intonation units in both registers. For others, like ABD, ARL and DCK, large differences between CDS and ADS, and remarkably fewer substantive units in CDS, can be seen.

Table 7.1: Substantive IUs in percentage of all utterances.

Age, ID	ADS	CDS
28, BLN	86.67	48.11
33, ABD	87.70	49.61
34, DCK	90.29	49.68
34, ARL	76.77	50.00
36, AMT	86.33	62.20
40, AVD	94.12	90.14
40, BCP	95.80	84.56
53, AGK	98.17	91.50
60, ALR	95.00	94.62
67, DCM	98.81	87.60

The difference between ADS and CDS correlates negatively with the age of the child, as a non-parametric Spearman correlation reveals ($r = -0.744$; $p = 0.014$) (see Figure 7.1). It is rather more necessary to regulate interactions with children than with adults, and the need intensifies the younger the children are. As Table 7.1 and Figure 7.1 show, there is not only a correlation, but also a clear boundary between the age of 36 and 40 months. Nearly half of what the younger children hear is regulatory IUs; from the age of 40 months on, there is a clear gap, such that only about 10 per cent of the intonation units addressed to children are regulatory. There are different reasons for adults to regulate interactions with a child, for example, by asking a lot of questions. Some children are extremely talkative, while others are very quiet or lacking in concentration. All of these individual styles can make it necessary for the narrator to regulate the interaction, as I describe in the following sections. For each function, there are different means used. The classic subdivision according to form does not seem appropriate for the current data as, for example, many questions are used with a directive function. Where possible and reasonable, statistical tests and descriptive measures will be added. If two children were present, the age of that child is used who was supposed to be the addressee, as it turned out that the regulatory intonation units are usually directed towards the intended listener.

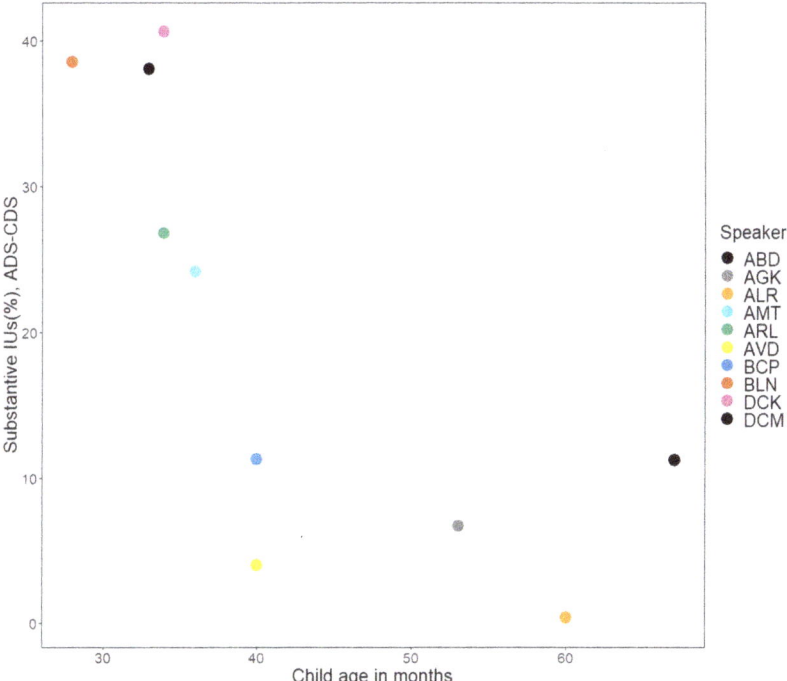

Figure 7.1: Substantive intonation units in per cent of all utterances correlated to the age of the children.

The few speech acts from the INCA-A that are rare in the data (e.g. declarations and promises) have been excluded from the investigation.

7.3 Functions of regulatory intonation units

7.3.1 Adults directing attention

Many imperatives are used in order to direct children's attention to the story. In Qaqet, imperatives are 'exclusively marked prosodically through a final rise […], and there are no dedicated imperative particles' (Hellwig 2019: 440). Hence, both speaker intent and intonation have been employed for the identification of imperatives in this study. See (53) with Figure 7.2 for an example of a typical Qaqet imperative and its fundamental frequency.

(53) *uannarli!*
      uan=narli
      2DU.SBJ=hear/feel
      'The two of you listen!' (PearAMTP 140)

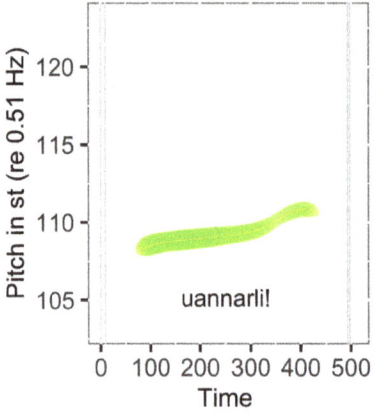

Figure 7.2: F₀-extraction for (53) (female speaker).

Attention may also be directed with reference to the direction of viewing: see (54) where BLN tells ZDL to look into her direction in order to get his attention.

(54) *nyinyim!*
      nyi=nyim
      SG.SBJ.NPST=look
      look! (PearBLNP00)

Some imperatives are used to silence children, as in example (55), while others again are used to control the children's physical behaviour, as in example (56). Nevertheless, all of those techniques are uttered with the same goal: namely, having the child quietly listen to the story.

(55) *sung nenyi de ...*
 sung ne-nyi de
 quiet from/with-2SG CONJ
 'be quiet and ...' (PearABDP 078)

(56) *nyaruqun nyaruqun!*
 nya=ruqun nya=ruqun
 2SG.SBJ=sit 2SG.SBJ=sit
 'sit down, sit down!' (PearABDP 143)

This explicit type of attention-directing is mostly found with younger children (see Table 7.3). Likewise, it is also younger children who hear more indirect imperatives, that is, polar questions with a directive function. Polar questions in Qaqet are built with the interrogative particle *kua* in utterance-initial position, as in (57). It is marked by a final rise-fall (see Figure 7.3).

(57) *kua uannarli?*
 kua uan=narli
 INTRG 2DU.SBJ=hear/feel
 'do you hear?' (PearABDP30)

While polar questions, as in (57), are a little less explicit than the imperatives, they still serve the same function. For both types, the same reaction on the part of the child satisfies the narrators. In (57), for example, the children do not answer, but they both look at ABD, and this is sufficient for her to continue her story. Polar questions like in (58) seem to superficially elicit answers relating to the content. However, they are used very much like the ones directly assessing the child's attention. As a reaction to AGK's question in (58), WMN shakes her head in affirmation[1] and AGK continues her story.

(58) *ali nyitlu?*
 i=lira nyi=tlu
 SIM=just_now 2SG.SBJ.NPST=see
 'Did you see?' (PearAGKP 007)

---

1 Qaqet shake their heads for confirming.

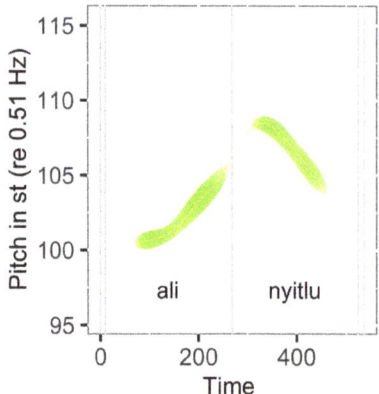

Figure 7.3: F_0-extraction for (58) (female speaker).

The same intentions may also be expressed by several other types of formatives, all shown in (59). DCK uses seven attention-directing utterances in sequence, as he tries to make his daughter ZEA listen. These are of different types: In lines (59a) and (59b) he uses a polar question as an implicit directive, then elicits confirmation of this with a tag question in line (59b) as she still does not react. In line (59c) he uses an imperative. In lines (59d), (59e) and (59g) he uses the interjection *sss* 'Hey!' and in line (59f) he calls her name to get her attention.

(59)   a.   DCK: *kua nyi narli?* 'do you hear?'
       b.   DCK: *da?* 'true?'
       c.   DCK: *nyinyim!* 'look here!'
       d.   DCK: *sss* 'sss'
       e.   DCK: *sss* 'sss'
       f.   DCK: *Ani!* 'Ani!'
       g.   DCK: *sss* 'sss' (PearDCKP 75-81)

The tag-question as used in (59b) is built by inserting the particle *da* 'right' at the end of an utterance to elicit confirmation from the hearer (Hellwig 2019: 442). Frequently, though, in the pear corpus it stands on its own, separated by a pause from the utterance to be confirmed (see (60)).

(60)   a.   *katramagam nadaamemgga*
             ka=tat=ama=gam
             3SG.M.SBJ=take/pick_up=ART=seed/fruit
             ne=de=aa=meng-ka
             from/with=LOC.PART=3SG.M.POSS=tree/wood-NC.SG.M
             'He picks fruit from the tree' (ABDP 26-27)

b. *da?*
   da
   true
   'True?' (PearABDP 26-27)

Five adult speakers made use of tag-questions. Most instances of the tag question occur directly after the adult has asked a polar question related to the attention of the child, usually 'Did you see …' or 'Do you hear …' (see Table 7.2). Adults use it to elicit a reaction from the children. As Table 7.2 shows, they do not insist on this answer. Only 10 of the 17 tag-questions are answered (even non-verbally) by the children, but the adults continue with their story nonetheless.

Table 7.2: Distribution of tag-questions in the pear corpus.

Total tag-questions (TQ)	22
TQ following a polar question (PQ)	18
TQ following an unanswered PQ	17
TQ answered (non-verbally) by child	10

The content question, finally, is built with the help of question words that appear in the position of the constituent in question (Hellwig 2019: 442). Some question words are illustrated in (61) (*gi* 'what') and (62) (interrogative verb *sana* 'do_what').

(61) *nyitlu amagiqa?*
nyi=tlu   ama=gi-ka
2SG.SBJ.NPST=see   ART=what-NC.SG.M
'What do you see?' (PearAGKP 009)

ABD uses a wide range of question words with her children: *gi* 'what', *sana* 'do what', *kesna* 'how much' and *nema* 'who'. She tells the pear story to two children: XCL (33m) who is supposed to be the primary addressee, and ZGT (72m), who joins them in the task. In (62), as she poses the question, she leans over to young XCL and tries to catch his gaze:

(62) *lira untlamaqaqeraqa iqesana?*
lira   un=tlu   ama=qaqet-ka   i=ke=sana
just_now   IDU=see   ART=person-NC.SG.M   SIM=3SG.M.SBJ.NPST=do_what
'Just now we saw the man and he did what?' (PearABDP 011)

Still, as XCL does not answer the question, she changes the direction of her gaze towards his elder brother and repeats the question. When ZGT answers, first she expands his answer like in (63), then she turns towards XCL again, asking him whether he has seen that, too (see (63d)), thereby pulling him into the conversation again. ABD does not accept XCL's slight headshake as a reaction (63e) but insists on a verbalisation. As he does not answer, she tries to elicit speech from him by asking repeatedly *aginget?* 'What is it?' (63f). At last, XCL whispers *agam* 'fruits' and ABD accepts and confirms this (63h).

(63) a. ABD: *kesana?* [turning her gaze towards ZGT]
 ke=sana
 3SG.M.SBJ.NPST=do.what
 'What does he do?'

 b. ZGT: *tramagam*
 tat ama=gam
 take/pick_up ART=seed/fruit
 'Pick fruits'

 c. ABD: *katramagam*
 ka=tat ama=gam
 3SG.M.SBJ=take/pick_up ART=seed/fruit
 'He picks fruits'

 d. ABD: *XCL! kua lira nyitlamaqaqera iqatramagam?*
 XCL kua lira
 name where/why just_now
 nyi=tlu ama=qaqera
 2SG.SBJ.NPST=see ART=person
 i=ka=tat ama=gam
 CONJ=3SG.M.SBJ=take/pick_up ART=seed/fruit
 'XCL! Did you see the man picking fruits?'

 e. XCL: [slightly shakes his head for confirmation]

 f. ABD: *aginget? aginget? aginget?*
 a=gi-nget a=gi-nget
 NM=thingy-NC.N NM=thingy-NC.N
 a=gi-nget
 NM=thingy-NC.N
 'what is it? what is it? what is it?'

 g. XCL: [whispers] *agam* a=gam
 NM=seed/fruit
 'fruits'

h. ABD: *ee, agam*
ee   a=gam
yes   NM=seed/fruit
'yes, fruits' (PearABDP 13-23)

As shown, although it takes time to elicit the answer to a content question from XCL, she does not give up until he answers. ABD uses by far the most content questions of all narrators. Content questions are associated with cognitive intentions and are rather typical of Western, urban societies (Vogt et al. 2015). ABD's frequent use of them could be an effect of her training and daily work as an elementary teacher, as it is her job to have children answer content questions.

All of the formatives described so far are used by adults in different proportions, see Table 7.3. There are some adults who make much use of the attention-directing devices while others do not. Only the number of imperatives and other formatives correlates negatively with the age of the listening child (Spearman-test; $r = -0.732$; $p = 0.016$), while the other variables do not. While imperatives and interjections like *sss* or calling a child's name are used primarily with younger children, there is no such connection for the other formatives. In order to explain the differences, I will describe the individual interactive style of the children in Section 7.3.2.

Table 7.3: Attention-directing speech acts in CDS: Imperative (Imp), Tag Questions, Polar Questions and Content Questions (Q).

Age, ID	Imp	Tag Q	Polar Q	Cont Q	Other
28, BLN	3	1	0	1	2
34, ARL	2	0	0		
34, DCK	11	24	14		15
40, AVD	1	0	1		
40, BCP		17	12		1
44, AMT	3	1	1		2
53, ABD	5	30	10	16	2
53, AGK		6	4		
60, ALR	1	0	0		1
67, DCM	1	9	5	0	
Total	27	88	47	17	23

7.3.2 Children signalling attention

There are three formatives the children use to signal attention. One of these is the tag-question. The use of tag-questions by children though differs a little from how adults use it. See (64) below for an instance of a tag-question produced by a child. The mother BLN tells the story to her 28-month-old son ZDL. The two have a backchannelling routine that can be seen in (64): utterances by BLN are commented upon by ZDL with a *da?* 'true?', to which BLN reacts with a mumbled *mm* 'yes'.

(64) a. BLN: *deqanes aagatim amaqunasim*
de   ka=nes
CONJ 3SG.SBJ=put_inside
aa=gata-im   ama=qunas-im
3SG.M.POSS=basket-NC.DU.F ART=one-NC.DU.F
'And he filled the two baskets'

b. ZDL: *da?*
da
right
'Really?'

c. BLN: *mm*
mm
yes
'Yes' (PearBLNP 21-24)

Although both adults and children use the tag question to elicit confirmation (Hellwig 2019: 442), adults use it to ensure that they have the children's attention, while children use it as a backchannelling device, to show by themselves that they are concentrated on the interaction. Another way that children do this is by asking for the location of things. Often, the question word *kua* 'where' is used. It occurs in the clause-final adverbial slot (Hellwig 2019: 443), as in (65) below. Here *ngulu* 'I see' at the beginning of the clause is part of the routine with *kua* 'where'. Still, the *ngulu* 'I see' can also be omitted like in (66).

(65) *ngulamagulengga qua?*
ngu=lu   ama=guleng-ka   kua
1SG.SBJ.NPST=see ART=malay_apple-NC.SG.M where
'Where is the malay apple?' (PearAMTP 094)

(66) *agam kua?*
      aa=gam   kua
      3SG.M.POSS=seed/fruit where
      'Where is the fruit?' (PearARLP 004)

The word *ngulu* 'I see' appears to be undergoing grammaticalisation as a question particle, like *kua*. In (67b) below, YDS leaves the *kua* 'where' out and uses only *ngulu* to ask for the location.

(67) a. AMT: *katigis aaiang amaguleng*
              ka=tigis   aa=ia-nget
              3SG.M.SBJ=pluck   3SG.M.POSS=other-NC.N
              ama=guleng
              ART=malay_apple
              'He picks some malay apples again'
     b. YDS: *ngulu?*
              ngu=lu
              1SG.SBJ.NPST=see 'Where?'
     c. YRA: *ngulamagulengga qua?*
              ngu=lu   ama=guleng-ka
              1SG.SBJ.NPST=see   ART=malay_apple-NC.SG.M
              kua
              where/why
              'Where is the malay apple tree?'
     d. AMT: *kemerama laptop*
              ke=met=ama=laptop
              3SG.M.SBJ.NPST=in=ART=laptop
              'On the laptop' (PearAMTP 92-96)

A third formative used to signal attention is to imitate the end of the previous adult utterance, which has already been described in Section 6.2.1. In most cases it is the last word or the last few words that are taken up by the children. The imitations by children are uttered with a final rise-fall intonation contour, signalling a polar question (Hellwig 2019: 54), as can be seen in (68) and with Figure 7.4, where YMN echoes the previous words of her father AVD. Usually, as AVD does, the adults confirm the question.

(68) a. AVD: *keksik lungura*
              ke=ksik   lu-nget-a
              3SG.M.SBJ.NPST=climb   DEM-NC.N-DIST
              'he climbs to pick those'

b. YMN: *lungula?*
   lu-nget-a
   DEM-NC.N-DIST
   'those?'

c. AVD: *mm*
   mm
   yes
   'yes' (PearAVDP 39-40)

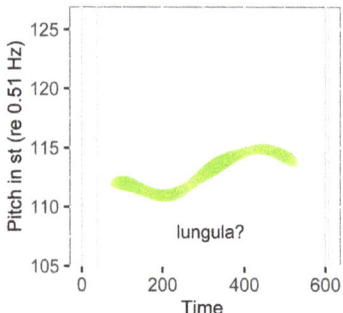

Figure 7.4: F0-extraction for (68 b.) (male speaker).

Several children make use of one or more of those techniques to signal attention, while others do not at all (see Table 7.4). In the next section, I connect the children's interactive style to the adults' attention-directing techniques.

7.3.3 Attention in interaction

In this chapter, I have shown that adults have several techniques to direct children's attention, and likewise that children have different methods to signal their attention.

A Spearman correlation showed that these two forms of verbal behaviour (sum of attentionals in CDS and sum of child's actions signalling attention) correlate negatively with each other ($r = -0.762$, $p = 0.01$). The more a child signals that she listens to what the adult says, the fewer attention directives the adults use.

The relationship between the two variables (ADS attention-directives and CDS attention-signals) can explain the high individual differences. In Figure 7.5, this relationship is clearly visible: until the age of 40 months, a low amount of child attentionals produces a high amount of adult attentionals.

Table 7.4: Backchannelling from children.

Age, ID	Tag Q	Where Q	Imitation
28, BLN	27	1	10
34, ARL	3	25	18
34, DCK			
40, AVD	1		12
40, BCP			1
44, AMT	14	4	25
53, ABD			
53, AGK			
60, ALR			4
67, DCM			
Total	45	30	70

Therefore, I added the two variables up for each adult-child-pair into a variable that stands for the 'sum of attention-related interactions'. A Spearman-test showed that the correlation between the sum of interactions and child age is highly significant ($r = 0.857$, $p = 0.002$).

The data suggest that from around 35 months on, the sum of attentionals decreases steadily until around 45 months (see Figure 7.5). Adults direct children's attention if the child does not signal it in some way, but as the child matures, they stop doing so, regardless of children's backchannelling behaviour. There are no attention-directing devices in the ADS data, regardless of the adults' backchannelling behaviour. Adults are able to follow a narration without being reminded to do so and from a certain age on, the same is expected of children.

7.4 Summary: Fulfilling a common task

The above considerations support what has been proposed by Snow (1994) and Saxton (2009), namely that speakers (both men and women likewise) try to enable successful communication with immature listeners or, as is the case for the present data, to allow successful cooperation with them. The children's main task during the pear story narrations was to listen to the story, that is, to be attentive.

CHILD-DIRECTED SPEECH IN QAQET

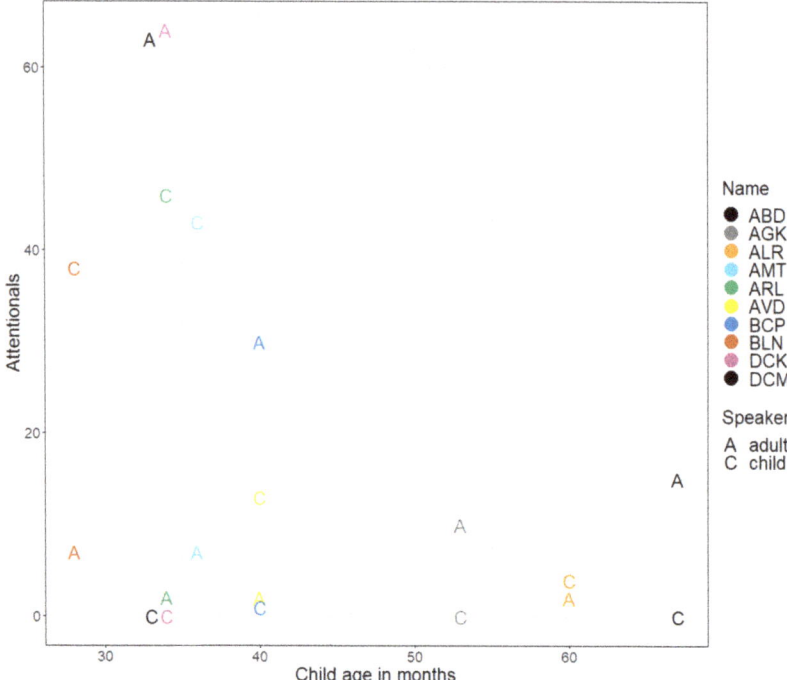

Figure 7.5: Attentionals by children (C) and adults (A) in comparison.

Having the children concentrate and, eventually, confirm that they are, is fulfilled by a range of different formatives in the Qaqet data. These lie on a continuum with respect to the (theoretically) expected reaction from the child, but adults often do not insist on the appropriate answer. The choice of one over the other seems to be an individual preference, although there is a tendency that the direct formatives are used with younger children.

It emerges from the data that adults are aware of the limited attentional capacities of children, and react by trying to direct their attention towards the interaction. They do so less frequently as the child reaches 35–45 months of age, assuming that children by then have acquired the capacity to concentrate on a given communicative interaction. Until that point, the more a child signals independently that he or she is attentive, the fewer attention-directing speech acts are required from the narrator. The relationship between the number of formatives and child age is mediated by children's backchannelling behaviour. From the age of around 40 months on, the adult data suggests that backchannelling behaviour is not related to attention-directing utterances any more.

8

Corrective input

8.1 Previous research on corrective input

This section deals with adults' comments on children's non-target-like linguistic productions. There is a broad literature on adults' reactions to non-target-like child utterances and the extent to which they are helpful for children's language acquisition. Explicit corrections by adults are more related to the meaning of children's utterances than to their form (Brown & Hanlon 1970). Adults tend to react with different forms of recasts (repetitions with corrections) to children's errors, which can serve as negative evidence for the children, and can positively influence their course of acquisition (Farrar 1990). Saxton (1997) found that this is especially the case when those utterances are presented directly after the child's error. In their longitudinal study of children acquiring English and French, Chouinard and Clark (2003) reported as much as 65 per cent of child errors to be directly followed by recasts. The rates were similar across different types of errors (phonological, morphological, syntactic and lexical). Less effective is negative feedback such as clarification questions (Saxton 2015). Opposed to negative evidence, negative feedback does not model the correct form. However, for both forms of feedback, there is not much research for non-WEIRD languages. Nevertheless, the existing research suggests that there is variation between language communities. Schieffelin (1990), for example, reports that Kaluli mothers use *elema* 'say it like this' to prompt the children to correct their non-target-like utterances, a much more explicit strategy. Explicit corrections are also what adults in Raunsepna report when they are asked how they correct children (Marley (2013); see Section 2.2.4). They expressed the opinion that children's errors have to be corrected, even if other people's children produce them and one happens to hear it (see (69)).

(69) *kuasik taqurlani, dap nyitaqan taqurlani*
kuasik   taquarl-ani,   dap nyi=taqen
NEG   like_this-DIST   but 2SG.SBJ.NPST=talk
taquarl-ani
like_this-DIST
'Do not talk like this, talk like that!' (AMS, Int_AMS_ARL)

However, they also describe a strategy like negative feedback as in the Tok Pisin utterance (70), which was provided as an example for me during the interviews (see Section 2.2.4).

(70) *Mi no save long hap tok hia yu tokim mi long em, yu tokim mi gut!*
'I do not know the word you said to me, tell me properly!'
(BCP, Int_BCP_ARN)

In her study on language use in Raunsepna, Marley (2013: 134) reported that the actual practice was very different from what speakers claimed in the interviews, with regard to correcting children. She presents preliminary evidence that indicates that clarification questions are the prevalent strategy.

8.2 Adults' reactions to non-target-like child utterances

8.2.1 Methods

For the current study, the corpus was searched for errors (in grammar, lexicon or pronunciation) produced by children. These were identified with the help of transcribers' judgements. However, there are quite a few child utterances that were excluded because they were not intelligible at all, or they were ignored by the adults. In other cases, it was not clear what type of error was produced by the child, as in example (71b) below. It is not clear if XAT was trying to imitate his father or produces something entirely different. None of the transcribers, among them ARL and XAT's mother, AMS, had any idea what *apelki* means, but ARL assumed it was an unsuccessful imitation of *hoski* 'horse'.

(71) a. ARL: *de kena.. kenama.. hoski*
 de ke=ne
 CONJ 3SG.M.SBJ.NPST=from/with
 ke=ne=ama=hos-ki
 3SG.M.SBJ.NPST=from/with=ART=horse-NC.SG.F
 'with.. with a.. with a horse'
 b. XAT: *apelki*
 ?
 ?
 c. ARL: *hoski!*
 hos-ki
 horse-NC.SG.F
 'Horse!' (PearARLP 13-15)

8.2.2 Approval and ignoring

In the whole corpus, there are 28 non-target-like utterances produced by children. All but two of these are instances of unsuccessful imitation. Table 8.1 shows adults' reactions to these child utterances. There are three types of reactions: mostly, adults ignore the child's utterance altogether, or they express approval while ignoring the form. Only three adults provide negative evidence by recasting the children's utterance. I will illustrate these types of reactions with reference to examples.

Table 8.1: Adults' reactions to non-target-like child utterances.

Adult Reaction	Instances	Speaker code
Approve	14	ARL, AVD, BLN
Ignore	8	AVD, DCM
Recast	6	ABD, ARL, BLN, AMT

In (72), YMN tries to repeat the last parts of her father's utterance. Instead of the correct form *angerlmamga* 'father' she produces *aemga*. Nevertheless, AVD agrees with *mm* 'yes'.

(72) a. AVD: *ma.. iaqama.. angerlmamga*
 ma ia-ka ama
 thus other-NC.SG.M ART
 a=ngerlmam-ka
 NM=man/father-NC.SG.M
 'So the.. the other.. man'

b. YMN: *aemga?*
a=ngerlmam-ka
man/father-NC.SG.M
'Man?'
c. AVD: *mm*
mm
YES
'Yes' (PearAVDP 002-004)

All similar instances are produced either by DCM or by AVD. In the pear task, children were not expected to be narrators. AVD and DCM might therefore consider it inappropriate to take notice of what the children say. A talkative child, then, may be silenced with a quick confirmation like in example (72). This is supported by the fact that the two men are also the only ones explicitly prompting their child listeners to be silent (see (73) and (74)).

(73) *sung nanyi dengusiit banyi!*
sung   ne-nyi   de=ngu=siiit
quiet   from/with-2SG   CONJ=1SG.SBJ=tell.story
barek-nyi
ben-2sg
'Be quiet so I can tell you the story!' (PearAVDP 005)

(74) *askerl kurli denyatu giasdem da?*
as=kerl   kurli   de=nya=tu
still=DEONT   stay/leave   CONJ=2SG.SBJ=put
gia=sdem   da
2SG.POSS=ear   true
'Leave it and listen, okay?' (PearDCMP 086)

Another method to deal with unwanted child productions is evidenced in (75). YMN unsuccessfully repeats her father's utterance *deqamrirl sanget* by echoing *mesamet*. AVD nevertheless continues his story without further comment on his daughter's incorrect production.

(75) a. AVD: *deqamrirl sanget*
            de=ka=mrirl   se-nget
            CONJ=SG.M.SBJ=descend   to/with-3N
            'And he descends with them'

b. YMN: *mesamet?*
     mrirl   se-nget
     descend   to/with-3N
     'Descends with them?'
c. AVD: *deqesnes met luqiama.. amaratki*
     de=ke=snes   met
     CONJ=3SG.M.SBJ.NPST=put_inside   in
     lu-ki-a   ama
     DEM-NC.SG.F-DIST   ART
     ama=rat-ki
     ART=basket-NC.SG.F
     'they put it into this.. the basket' (PearAVDP 025-027)

Approval and ignoring are the most frequent adult reactions to child errors in the corpus. However, some adults do provide negative evidence in the form of recasts.

8.2.3 Recast

Table 8.2 shows the recasts per speaker and the type of child error they relate to. Only four adult speakers use recasts; their child listeners produce 23 out of the 28 errors present in the corpus.

Table 8.2: Recast per speaker and type of non-target-like form produced by the children.

Speaker Code	Expansions	Type of non-target-like utterance
ABD	1	pronoun choice
AMT	1	omission/pronunciation
ARL	2	omission, pronunciation
BLN	2	omission, preposition choice

In this section, I will provide an example of each type of error, the adult uptake, and child reaction to this. Occasionally, the type of error is not entirely clear, see, for example, (76): ARL models the correct pronunciation of the sentence for his son XAT after XAT tries to imitate him. XAT's production is an imperfect echo of the target produced by ARL. ARL repeats every part of his utterance separately, and XAT then imitates him again. Still, in (76f) he is not able to pronounce *nara*, but instead says *lara*. This time, though, ARL simply continues with his story, ignoring the non-target-like pronunciation. XAT is the only child who tries to repeat the correct form modelled for him.

(76) a. ARL: *amadepguas nara*
 ama=depguas ne-ta
 ART=three from/with-3PL.H
 'Three of them'
 b. XAT: **demgarara?**
 ama=depguas ne-ta
 ART=three from/with-3PL.H
 'Three of them?'
 c. ARL: *adepguas!*
 a=depguas
 NM=three
 'Three!'
 d. XAT: *adepguas?*
 a=depguas
 SPEC=three
 'Three?'
 e. ARL: *nara!*
 ne-ta
 from/with-3PL.H
 'Of them!'
 f. XAT: *lara?*
 ne-ta
 from/with-3PL.H
 'Of them?' (PearARLP 107-111)

In (77), ABD models the right form for her son ZGT who leaves out the subject clitic *ka* '3sg.m.sbj'. After she corrects him this way, she does not insist on a reaction from him, but turns her attention directly towards younger XCL.

(77) a. ABD: *kesana?*
 ke=sana
 3SG.M.SBJ.NPST=do_what
 'What does he do?'
 b. ZGT: *tramagam*
 tat ama=gam
 take/pick_up ART=seedfruit
 'Pick fruits'
 c. ABD: *katramagam!*
 ka=tat ama=gam
 3SG.M.SBJ=take/pick_up ART=seed/fruit
 'He picks fruits!'

d. ABD: *XCL!*
          XCL
          NAME
          'XCL!' (ABDP 13-16)

Another instance of a grammar-related recast of a child's utterance is illustrated in (78). ZDL imitates his mother's utterance using the non-target-like preposition (*de* 'loc' instead of *met* 'in') and BLN models the right expression for him. ZDL does not repeat what she told him, and answers instead with the tag-question *da?* 'true?', but BLN nevertheless agrees with an affirmative *mm*.

(78) a. BLN: *davaaiaik dequasik metki*
             dap   aa=ia-ki
             but   3SG.M.POSS=other-NC.SG.F
             de=kuasik met-ki
             CONJ=NEG in-3SG.F
             'But the other one there was nothing inside'
     b. ZDL: *da?*
             da
             right
             'Really?'
     c. BLN: *mm*
             mm
             yes
             'Yes'
     d. ZDL: *kuasik demgi?*
             kuasik   de-ki
             NEC   LOC.PART-3SG.F
             'Nothing there?'
     e. BLN: *kuasik metki!*
             kuasik   met-ki
             NEG   in-3SG.F
             'Nothing inside'
     f. ZDL: *da?*
             da
             right
             'Really?'
     g. BLN: *mm*
             mm
             yes
             'Yes' (BLNP 158-162)

Before I summarise the results from this chapter in Section 8.3, I will present a last example indicating that recasting might not be the only way to correct in Qaqet. While feedback to non-target-like child utterances is, if at all, only provided in the form of recasts, there are two examples of negative feedback related to an inaudible utterance produced by the child, both produced by ABD. In (79), ABD asks her son about the fruits on the tree from the film. His answer is too low in volume; therefore, she repeats the same question again to show that she did not hear her son's utterance. As he repeats it louder but omits the obligatory article, she agrees and recasts his utterance, adding the omitted form.

(79) a. ABD: *aginget?*
a=gi-nget
NM=thingy-NC.C
'What are they?'
b. XCL: *[inaudible]*
?
?
c. ABD: *aginget?*
a=gi-nget
NM=thingy-NC.N
'What are they?'
d. XCL: *[whispering] gam*
gam
seed/fruit
'Fruits'
e. ABD: *ee, agam*
ee a=gam
yes nm=seed/fruit
'Yes, fruit'

8.3 Summary: Imitation and recast

The current chapter has demonstrated that most child errors are produced when children try to imitate adults' productions. In Section 6.2.1, I introduced the children's habit of imitating the ends of adults' utterances by turning them into polar questions. In Section 7.3.2, I discussed the imitation routine as a form of backchannelling behaviour used by children to signal that they are listening to the adult narrator. The evidence from the current chapter suggests that imitation is also used as a form of negative feedback, signalling the children's need for clarification.

Despite the reports of explicit correction by adults from Raunsepna, there are no instances of those found in the pear corpus. This supports previous research that suggests this form of feedback is infrequent (Brown & Hanlon 1970).

Opposed to evidence from other languages, however, most non-target-like forms of children are ignored (Chouinard & Clark 2003). Likewise, many adults answer with affirmatives, regardless of erroneous linguistic form. This is partly explained by the roles of adults as speakers and children as listeners during the pear task. It also confirms previous evidence from other languages suggesting that adults often react to the content, rather than the linguistic form, of children's utterances (Brown & Hanlon 1970).

However, if adults notice and comment on child errors, they do this by recasting the children's utterance in a correct form. There are six of these instances following different types of non-target-like child productions, both in grammar and pronunciation. Among the children, only XAT repeats the modelled forms. ZDL, instead, reacts with tag-questions. The narrators do not or approve explicitly, but they tend to just continue their stories.

In addition to the recasts following child errors, negative feedback is used by one woman to signal that she did not understand what her child said. ABD uses clarification requests following inaudible child utterances and her children repair those by speaking louder. While witnessed only twice in the current data, these instances are still an indication that this technique exists in Qaqet CDS. In a larger corpus, it might appear as feedback towards non-target-like child utterances.

To summarise, I have presented evidence on negative evidence and negative feedback in Qaqet CDS. Moreover, I have shown that children are sensitive to those forms of feedback. Adults (both male and female) correct different non-target-like forms produced by children, although most of these are ignored. This can be explained considering the children's role as listeners in this study.

Speakers' reports of their language practice are only partly congruent with what they actually do. In line with Marley's (2013) observation, speakers report that they correct children in an explicit manner, but the actual corrections found in the data are rather implicit. A similar discrepancy will be discussed again in Chapter 9 on special forms in the lexicon.

9
CDS and the Qaqet lexicon

9.1 Previous research on special babytalk words

A special CDS-vocabulary has been documented for many languages. For example, Ferguson (1964) reported reduplicated lexemes for use with babies in the lexicons of Syrian Arabic, Marathi, Comanche, Gilyak, American English and Spanish. He hypothesises that this 'can probably be regarded as a feature of baby talk throughout the world' (Ferguson 1964: 109). Richards and Gallaway (1994) analyse baby talk words as an imitation of children's early productions. These are used by adults possibly in order to facilitate comprehension for children. Sarvasy (2019/01/25), for instance, reports the mimicking of phonetic features of babies' speech in Nungon, a language of Papua New Guinea. For the Baining language Mali, Stebbins reports a set of baby talk words with a mostly CV(C) syllable structure. Among the 15 baby talk words she presents, eight have the reduplicated form CVC-CVC, for example, [kak$kak] 'maternal uncle' instead of the adult word [kau] (Stebbins 2011: 29).

For convenience, I briefly recall adults' comments on baby talk reported in Chapter 2. While Qaqet adults confirm that they know baby talk words, the use of them is stigmatised, and considered to provide children with a bad example. Baby talk is considered an imitation of the imperfect child language, but several interviewees admit that it might be used for facilitative or instructional purposes. There are only few words people mention, the most frequent among them being *tata* 'delicious food, meat'. The Tok Pisin form *susu* 'breastfeed' is frequently used towards small children in the form *tutu*. Similarly, the Qaqet word *sup* 'drink' is realised as *tup* when used in child-directed imperatives. Among these examples, the latter two are especially relevant in communication with infants who are still being breastfed, mostly as a way to soothe the child. Their form is typical for the kind of baby talk described by Ferguson (1964): *tata* and *tutu* consist of a single reduplicated syllable. For *tutu* and *tup* the baby talk form differs from the adult form in the realisation of fricatives as plosives.

9.2 Babytalk words in the CDS-pear stories

In the data from the pear stories, there are few specific lexical forms. Sets of baby talk words are often found for semantic domains that are typical for infants' everyday life (Ferguson 1964). Nevertheless, there are some words the transcribers identified as baby talk in one pear story told by ARL to his son XAT (34m) while AMS, the mother, was sitting close by.

Example (80) shows how XAT reacts with an imitative polar question to ARL's utterance *saiqeqiuaik*, but instead of producing *qiuaik* 'run' in the continuous form like his father, he uses a reduplicated version of the noncontinuous form *uaik* [waik]. He repeats the consonant [w] plus the diphthong [ai], and the coda [k] finishes the word. So from a C1V1C2 word, he creates a C1V1C1V1C2 word.

(80) a. ARL: *saiqeqiuaik*
saqi=ke=qiuaik
again/also=3SG.M.SBJ.NPST=run
'He runs again'
b. XAT: *saiqauaiuaik?*
saqi=ka=uaiuaik
again/also=3SG.M.SBJ=run:REDUPL
'He runs again?' (PearARLP 132-133)

Several turns later, see (81), XAT signals that he has not understood an utterance produced by AMS, asking two times *ah?* 'what?'. AMS does not repeat the verb *tit* 'go' she used before, but instead uses the reduplicated form she heard before in (80) from XAT. The transcribers commented the form *uaiuaik* 'run:redupl' was a form used by and with babies to improve understanding.

(81) a. AMS: *saiqatit*
           saqi=ka=tit
           again/also=3SG.M.SBJ=go
           'He goes, too'
     b. XAT: *ah?*
           ah
           what
           'What?'
     c. ARL: *iva..*
           ip-a
           CONJ-DIST
           'Afterwards..'
     d. XAT: *ah?*
           ah
           what
           'What?'
     c. AMS: *kauaiuaik* ka=uaiuaik
           3SG.M.SBJ=run:REDUPL
           'He runs' (PearARLP 157)

Several turns later in the same session (see 82), XAT again signals that he has not understood a verb used by ARL, namely *ual* 'whistle'. ARL then repeats his utterance (82c) and XAT imitates it successfully (82d), which is confirmed by ARL.

(82) a. ARL: *saiakaual*
           saqi=ia-ka=ual
           again/also=other-3SG.M=whistle
           'The other one whistles'
     b. XAT: *ah?*
           ah
           what
           'What?'
     c. ARL: *saiak kelual*
           saqi=ia-ka=lual
           again/also=other-3SG.M=whistle
           'The other one whistles'
     d. XAT: *kaual?*
           ka=ual
           3sg.m.sbj=whistle
           'He whistles?'

e. ARL: *ee*
ee
yes
'Yes' (PearARLP 134-137)

Later yet in the same session, XAT demonstrates his newly acquired vocabulary. He reduplicates the verb *ual* 'whistle', (see (83)), producing *ualual* 'whistle:REDUPL'. His mother takes this up and repeats it whispering, possibly addressing his father who seems irritated by his son's comments. However, as XAT continues to repeat his utterance, his mother tells him to be quiet.

(83) a. AMS: *akaualual*
ia-ka=ualual
other-3SG.M.SBJ=whistle:redupl
'The other whistles'
b. XAT: *akaualual*
ia-ka=ualual
other-3SG.M.SBJ=whistle:redupl
'The other whistles'
c. (something happens)
d. AMS: *XAT, sung nanyi denyinarli!*
sung   ne-nyi
quiet   from/with-2SG
de=nyi=narli
CONJ=2SG.SBJ.NPST=hear/feel
'XAT, be quiet and listen' (PearARLP 215-223)

The examples from this single story suggest that reduplication is a typical baby talk form in at least one family in Raunsepna. XAT is able to use the technique of reduplication productively, and his mother imitates him when he signals that he does not know a word used by his father. However, the phenomenon might indeed be family specific. There are no similar occurrences in the other pear stories.

9.3 Summary

There are only three examples that people refer to as typical for baby talk and they consider them to imitate young babies' productions. These involve reduplication and the realisation of fricatives as plosives. The former is mentioned, among others, by Ferguson (1964) as a typical feature of baby talk. Likewise, fricatives are difficult to produce; therefore, their realisation as plosives possibly makes it easier for children to pronounce them. Reduplication is also used by AMS towards her son XAT, probably in an attempt to facilitate his comprehension. However, the marked absence of those forms in the other pear stories could be a result of adults' negative view of those forms. Likewise, the child participants could be too old for nursery vocabulary. The controlled content makes it even less likely to find these words in the pear corpus. Yet, the presence of a few instances gives rise to the hypothesis that there might be more such forms, possibly even differing between individual families. The amount of variation between individuals and families is one of the issues I discuss in the following conclusion.

10

Conclusion

10.1 Hypothesis

This study is based on previous research that has shown that child-directed speech is a separate register in many languages that differs systematically from adult-directed speech on various levels of linguistic description. Yet, there is growing evidence of the amount of variation between different speech communities, especially with regard to the amount of directed speech children receive, but also regarding the interactional, linguistic and conceptual features of that speech. Variation in ideologies, socio-economic situation and the personality of children and caregivers are only some of the factors that influence children's input. Notably, there are large differences between WEIRD societies and small-scale rural societies.

Based on previous research on the language input of children in such contexts, I expected to find a low level of CDS and a set of attitudes towards child learning to interact with this level. Previous evidence points to the probability that CDS, if present, would show a 'range of modifications' (Gallaway & Richards 1994: 257). For example, a high number of directives and a low number of questions have been described for small-scale, subsistence-based contexts. Thus, I assumed that regardless of the amount of input children receive, this input would be structurally different from the language used towards adults.

10.2 Socio-economic background

In Section 2.2.2, I described the non-linguistic aspects of children's everyday lives. The Qaqet in Raunsepna are a fairly typical small-scale rural community. Most people live by subsistence-based farming, and formal education is not of central importance in the lives of many villagers. Children are socialised from early on into their roles as adults in such a society. They are given responsibility for various everyday tasks from an early age, and sibling caregiving is common. The leading principle of socialisation is communal action autonomy (Keller 2007), favouring the well-being of the community and physical development rather than individual psychological autonomy. In general, children are perceived as self-initiative learners and have a high level of autonomy. In Section 2.2.3, I presented evidence for the existence of various types of toys and child play among the Qaqet Baining of Raunsepna. Opposing previous claims, I showed that play is neither suppressed nor devalued by adults; rather, some Qaqet even highlight various possible benefits from child play.

10.3 Language attitudes

The ideologies towards language socialisation reported in the interview study (Section 2.2.4) resemble those reported by Casillas et al. (2020a) for Rossel Islanders. Speaking to children is valued among many adults in Raunsepna, who emphasise the importance of talking to children, even to small babies. Some highlight the emotional bonding or the instructional effect. Both mother and father are responsible for a proper language development. However, while people also mention the positive effects of modifications in child-directed language, there are some skeptical voices. Some perceive it as 'false evidence', and several people say that only mothers, but not fathers, would adapt their speech to children. The evidence from the narrative corpus documents the opposite: all of the differences between ADS and CDS appear in fathers' and mothers' language alike. This inconsistency can be explained by referencing different concepts of CDS: most interviewees referred only to phonetic simplification of words for breastfeeding, which may well be restricted to mothers. A reduced utterance length, on the contrary, is mentioned by several participants as necessary for successful communication with small children. Furthermore, interviewees emphasise the importance of correcting children's non-target-like utterances, and provide examples of explicit corrections. Similar to the findings for other languages, there are no instances of explicit corrections in the CDS data, and many non-target-like utterances are not corrected. When they are, adults most likely use recasts to model the correct version. This happens with children of different ages, as opposed to other modifications that appear more time-bound.

In the introduction to this study, I referred to claims that research on CDS might offer insights into the mechanisms of language shift. In Chapter 2, I showed that while both Uramot Baining and Qaqet Baining feel shame with regard to child language perceived as 'incorrect', they react differently. Among the Uramot, people do not correct their children, while the Qaqet emphasise the necessity of doing so. A possible explanation might be the status of language shift in the two communities. In remote Raunsepna, people are proficient in their vernacular language, and feel sufficiently competent to correct non-target-like utterances. Thereby, they provide negative evidence for their children, which can then positively influence their language competence. In the more accessible Uramot community, however, people are not confident with respect to their language competence due to language shift. The public pressure stigmatising non-target-like language restrains them from correcting their children who, in turn, cannot learn to do better. Thus, the same attitude has different effects, depending on the advancement of language shift.

10.4 The amount of input

In Section 2.3, I presented the results of a pilot study on the amount of speech children in Raunsepna hear from their interlocutors. The amount of speech was comparable to the amount children in other rural, non-Western societies received. However, the data set I used was exceptionally small, and the differences between the children high. Still, the pilot study is consistent with the hypothesis that, with regard to the amount of CDS, the Qaqet community is comparable to other similar language communities.

Research from the paradigm of language socialisation highlighted the role of attitudes to children and child language for the children's language environment. My pilot study indicates that the situation (activity, participants, etc.) is of higher relevance not only with regard to the amount of input, but also with regard to its sources. These findings support the results by Casillas et al. (2020a), who found not ideologies, but rather the socio-economic situation predictive for the amount of input. They showed ideologies to be the relevant factor in predicting the interlocutors from whom children heard most input. For the children in my pilot study, the family's residential and socialising habits seem to be the relevant factors that determine who they interact with. Still, given the limitations of the study, additional factors are possible.

10.5 Structural features of Qaqet CDS

I used a stimulus-based production task to create two parallel sub-corpora, one for ADS and one for CDS. Those corpora have been compared for MLU (Chapter 4); number of disfluencies and position of hesitations (Chapter 5); mean fundamental frequency, total frequency range and speaking rate (Chapter 6); attention-organising utterances (Chapter 7); instances of corrections (Chapter 8); and dedicated baby talk lexemes (Chapter 9).

Typical features of CDS were found for all of these domains both in the language of male and female narrators when talking to children. Speaking rate was the only domain where CDS and ADS did not differ. Corrections, attention-organising utterances and few potential baby talk forms are only found in the child-directed stories and those told to adults. ADS and CDS also differ significantly in MLU, number of disfluencies and total frequency range. The difference between ADS and CDS furthermore correlates negatively with child age for MLU, mean fundamental frequency and the amount of attention-organising utterances.

10.5.1 Turning point for adaptations

The development of mean utterance length, mean fundamental frequency and attention-monitoring interactions in CDS is not gradual and linear. The difference between ADS and CDS in utterance length vanishes around 40 months of child age. The difference in mean fundamental frequency, however, is two semitones or larger before 40 months of child age and around one semitone for the older children. Similarly, 35–45 months is the age until which a high degree of attention-regulation occurs and only when the children themselves signal their attention: narrators do not direct them.

However, after 45 months, the adults in this study do not use many attentionals anymore, regardless of the children's communicative behaviour. These observations suggest that Qaqet adults perceive their child interlocutors to acquire a specific level of competence at the relevant age, making some sorts of adaptation unnecessary, or at least less necessary.

My results show that the age of children when this turning point is reached differs between languages and within languages and also depends on the relevant linguistic phenomenon. How the turning point interacts with other factors in child language acquisition remains to be investigated. I hope that my work will serve as a basis for future studies investigating the causes of such dynamics. Possibly, controlling for milestones in child (language) development, but also for cultural attitudes, activity type and language features would enhance our knowledge with regard to the different turning points in CDS.

10.5.2 Attention and comprehension

Some of the results are surprising in view of earlier research. For example, the largest total frequency ranges are found in the language directed towards the two oldest children. This coincides with a structural feature of Qaqet: the typical intonation contour positions the highest ranges utterance-finally. As the pitch movements are indications of turn-organisation in Qaqet, the frequency range emphasises discourse relevant features of utterances, even towards children older than five years. The ends of utterances, however, are not only highlighted by adults, but are also primarily attended to by children. This is evidenced by frequent imitations of the relevant parts by children in the form of clarification requests, which simultaneously signal to the adult that the child is focused on the interaction. Most adults, on the other hand, signal that they follow their child listeners' focus by responding to these questions. Sometimes, these adaptations provoke disfluencies when adults need additional processing time to find the adequate adaptations to the child's knowledge. While disfluencies have been described by earlier research as obstacles to children's language comprehension, recent work suggest that the opposite may be true. Even small children may read them as signals announcing complicated utterances that, in turn, shows them when special concentration is needed.

Adults monitored children's attention and level of competence. They adapted their language even to individual communicative styles. Many of the modifications found in Qaqet CDS have been described as potentially beneficial for children learning language; a low MLU, for example, reduces processing load, and a high mean fundamental frequency attracts children's attention and conveys affect.

In summary, both on the interactional level and on the linguistic level, there is clear evidence for the sort of input termed 'facilitative' or 'high quality' (Rowe & Snow 2020).

10.5.3 Cultural beliefs and individual variation

Several of the patters found in language use reflect the beliefs reported in the interviews. Those patterns indicate a set of culturally shared beliefs that influences actual language practice. For instance, adults' belief that children learn language by imitating their caregivers is reflected in children's imitation habits (see Section 6.2.1 and Section 7.3.2). Other examples include the 'where routine' and the 'fetching routine' (see Section 7.3.2 and Section 2.2.4), which provide linguistically framed pathways for the children into accepted forms of behaviour with reference to salient cultural concepts. The belief that parents are responsible for proper language acquisition is mirrored, for instance, in corrections of children's language (see Section 2.2.4 and Chapter 8).

Despite these tendencies, there is a considerable amount of interpersonal (or inter-family) variation. Different persons prefer different verbal means to fulfill the same function, or they use forms that are only known to their relatives. This is another topic that seems promising for future research: the interplay of speaker variables, such as family differences, educational level, or communicative style, with regard to the modifications that figure in CDS.

10.6 Limitations and future research

The present results are indicative of a separate, adaptive register of CDS in Qaqet. Yet, they have clear limitations. Retelling films is not a typical everyday activity that adults pursue together with their small children in Raunsepna. It may overemphasise linguistic and interactional features associated with an orientation towards cognitive intentions. Also, the nature of the task may have provoked adults to use a style towards older children that is usually reserved for younger ones. The ecological validity of the present results remains to be tested with longitudinal recordings of spontaneous interaction. Central questions emerging from this study are the amount of language directed towards young children in Qaqet and, especially, the nature of the language produced by other children towards young learners.

I hope this study is an indication of the variety of possible and helpful insights that the study of children's language environment in diverse communities offers. Yet, those opportunities decrease as a growing number of children cannot be granted the chance to acquire their own languages any more.

Appendix: Interview guideline and results

Table A.1: Statements and answers to the statements from the interviews.

Number	Yes	No	Statement
1	19	1	Ol pikinini i laik bihainim ol bikpela long wok. 'Children like to imitate adults' work.'
2	20	0	Long lainim, ol i lukluk long wok bilong ol bikpeka na bihainim ol. 'They watch the work of adults and do the same.'
3	20	0	Sampela pikinini i sa karai long sikirap taim ol i lukim mama sikirapim taro. 'Some children cry for a scraper if they see their mother scraping taro.'
4	19	1	Ol pikinini i sa karai long naip taim ol i lukim mama na papa wok wantaim naip. 'Some children cry for the knife when their parents work with the knife.'
5	19	0	Ol pikinini sa karai long karim bek taim ol i lukim ol bikpela karim bek. 'Some children cry for the bag when they see adults carrying the bag.'
6	20	0	Taim ol pikinini bihainim wok bilong mama na papa bilong ol, mama na papa mas strongim ol. 'When children imitate their parents' work, the parents must encourage them.'
7	18	2	Namba wan samting ol pikinini i lainim em karim paiawut, pasim paiawut na pulimapim wara. 'The first tasks of children are fetching firewood and fetching water.'
8	20	0	Ol pikinini i mas lain long wok gaden. 'The children have to learn garden work.'
9	20	0	Ol i lain long wit, long painim kaukau na kumu. 'They learn to weed and to find sweet potatoes and leafy greens.'

Number	Yes	No	Statement
10	20	0	*Save long karim ol samting nabaut long bus em bikpela samting long ol peles bilong ol Baining.* 'It is important to know how to carry cargo where the Bainings live.'
11	18	0	*Ol bikpela bilong em bai go wantaim em na em bai bihainim ol.* 'The older siblings go with the child and it follows their example.'
12	18	0	*Ol pikinini i mas lain long statim paia.* 'Children have to learn to start a fire.'
13	19	0	*Ol bikpela pikinini sa lukautim ol liklik.* 'Older siblings look after younger siblings.'
14	3	1	*Tude, ol pikinini stat long wok early; bipo, ol i bin statim wok taim ol i bikpela liklik, tasol nau, ol liklik stret stat long wok wantaim naip.* 'Today, childen start to work early in their lives. Before, they started to work later (as teens), but now, even the small ones work with knives.'
15	4	0	*Taim skul i bin kamap long Raunsepna, planti samting i senis long laip bilong ol pikinini. wanem samting?* 'When the school was built in Raunsepna, much changed in the life of children. (What changed?)'
16	3	0	*Bipo, ol bikpela i bin lukautim ol liklik. Nau ol bikpelai go long skul na planti ol liklik pikinini sa lukautim olliklik bilong ol.* 'Before, the older children watched about the younger ones. Now the older children go to school and often the small children watch about their younger siblings.'
17	16	0	*Taim ol i bikpela liklik, meri na man gat wok bilong ol yet.* When the children grow up, both boys and girls have their own work.
18	16	0	*Meri i lain long wit, planim na wok bilong haus na lukautim ol pikinini.* 'Girls learn to weed, to plant, to do the household and to take care for children.'
19	16	0	*Ol man i lain long klinim gaden, wokim banis na katim ol diwai.* 'Boys learn to clean the garden, to build fences and to cut trees.'
20	20	0	*Ol pikinini i mas pilai.* 'Children must play.'
21	18	0	*Taim ol i stat long wok, i olsem pilai: Ol i pilai wok na olsem ol i lainim hau ol bikpela sa wok.* 'When they start to work, it's like playing: They play that they work and that way they learn how the adults work.'
22	17	2	*Ol pikinini i lainim long wok taim ol i pilai.* 'Children learn to work while they play.'

APPENDIX

Number	Yes	No	Statement
23	15	3	*Sapos ol i no pilai, ol i no ken lainim wok bilong ol.* 'If they do not play, they cannot learn their work.'
24	11	5	*Olgeta mama na papa long olgeta kantri mas pilai long pikinini bilong ol.* 'All parents everywhere have to play with their children.'
25	19	0	*Sapos pilai bilong ol pikinini i kamap laut tumas na ol bikpela i laik toktok, ol pikinini mas go.* 'If children's play is getting too loud and the adults want to talk, the children have to go somewhere else.'
26	19	0	*Rispek em bikpela samting long lainim long ol pikinini long ol Baining.* 'Respect is important for the children of the Baining.'
27	19	0	*Taim ol narapela I lukim olsem wanpela pikinini i nogat rispek na I no save long wok, mama na papa bai sem.* 'If the other adults see that a child is not respectful and does not know how to work, the parents will be ashamed.'
28	18	0	*Sampela pikinini i sa raf nabaut long haus bilong ol yet, tasol taim ol I stap long haus bilong narapela ol bai gat bikpela rispek.* 'Some children behave very wild at home, but at other people's houses, they are very respectful.'
29	18	0	*Ol pikinini i mas lain long serim.* 'Children have to learn to share.'
30	14	2	*Sapos i gat wanpela bisket, bikpela pikinini mas givim long liklik pikinini.* 'If there is only one biscuit, the older children have to give it to the smallest child.'
31	16	0	*Taim ol bikpela i toktok, ol pikinini mas stap isi.* 'When adults are talking, children have to be quiet.'
32	19	0	*Ol pikinini i noken kurukutim lek bilong ol bikpela alain.* 'Children should not step over adults' legs.'
33	16	1	*Taim i gat visita long haus, ol pikinini noken ran nabaut na pilai.* 'If there are visitors, children cannot run around and play.'
34	15	1	*Ol pikinini noken disturb ol bikpela.* 'Children should not disturb the adults.'
35	17	2	*Sapos pikinini i no soim rispek, mama na papa mas paitim em. Olsem bai isi long em long lainim.* 'If children behave badly, the parents have to beat them. That way, the children will learn easily.'
36	20	0	*Long nambis, ol lain i sa kam long olgeta hap long PNG. Olsem, planti ol Baining i save Tok Pisin tasol.* 'Down at the coast, people come from all over PNG. That's why many Baining only talk Tok Pisin.'
37	20	0	*Taim ol i miks marit, ol lain i save Tok Pisin tasol.* 'If the people live in mixed marriages, they only use Tok Pisin.'

Number	Yes	No	Statement
38	19	1	*Sampela ol lain long nambis, maski mama na papa i Baining, i no save tokples long family.* 'Some people at the coast, although both spouses are Baining, do not use Tokples at home.'
39	20	0	*Sapos yu Baining, yu mas tokples Baining. Yu mas lainim ol pikinini bilong yu long Tokpes.* 'If you are Baining, you should use your own vernacular. You have to teach it to your children.'
40	14	0	*Planti ol lain bilong arasait i tok olsem: tokples Baining i hatwok.* 'Many people from elsewhere say: Baining language is difficult.'
41	18	0	*Yu mas lainim tokples pastaim, bihain Tok Pisin.* 'You have to learn your vernacular first, afterwards Tok Pisin.'
42	18	0	*Mama na Papa mas skulim ol pikinini bilong ol long tokples.* 'The parents have to teach their vernacular to their children.'
43	17	0	*Yu mas sa ve long tokples bilong yu bikos kastem i stap insait long tokples.* 'You have to know your vernacular because it is connected to your culture.'
44	17	0	*Em gutpela long save long Tok Pisin. Tasol tokples bilong yu i go pas.* 'It is good to know Tok Pisin, but your vernacular should come first.'
45	20	0	*Ol pikinini i sa lainim tokples bikos ol i kisim long maus bilong mama na papa.* 'Children learn their vernacular because they "take it from their parents' mouths".'
46	20	0	*Ol pikinini i sa harim mama na papa toktok na ol i bihainim.* 'Children listen to their parents as they speak and imitate them.'
47	18	0	*Taim yu gat wanpela bebi, yu hamamas long em na olsem yu laik toktok long em.* 'If you have a baby, you are happy about the baby and so you talk to him.'
48	19	0	*Ol pikinini, long lainim tokples, i mas harim planti toktok.* 'To learn their vernacular, children have to hear much speech.'
49	19	1	*Mama na papa na ol narapela long family mas toktok planti long ol bebi.* 'The parents and the others in the family have to talk much to the baby.'
50	19	0	*Mama na papa sa skulim ol pikinini olsem bai ol i bihainim.* 'The parents school their children and they imitate them.'
51	20	0	*Taim ol pikinini i stat long raun nabaut wantaim ol poroman na poromeri bilong ol, ol narapela pikininii skulim ol long tokples.* 'When children start to play with their friends, the other children teach them their language.'

Number	Yes	No	Statement
52	19	0	*Ol pikinini i sa kisim tokples hariap tru.* 'Children learn their vernacular very fast.'
53	18	0	*Planti ol fesbon i kisim tokples long maus bilong mama na papa. Ol narapela i sa kisim planti tokples long ol bikpela bilong ol.* 'Firstborn children learn from the parents, the other children learn much language from their older siblings.'
54	17	0	*Pastaim ol liklik bebi ol i no save long tokples.* 'When they are born, babies to not know their language.'
55	21	0	*Taim em i save pinis long wokabaut, ol lain bai tokim em: Go kisim ...! Olsem em bai save.* 'When children know how to walk, you can teach them like this: Go and fetch ... That way they'll learn.'
56	21	0	*Yu mas wokim eksen taim yu toktok long pikinini bilong yu.* 'You must use gestures when you talk to your child.'
57	21	0	*Yu ken skulim pikinini bilong yu olsem: Yu askim em "em wanem.." wantaim eksen.* 'You can teach your children like this: You ask them "Em wanem.. ?" accompanied by gestures.'
58	20	0	*Ol mama i save tanim toktok bilong ol taim ol i toktok long pikinini bilong ol.* 'Mothers change their speech when they are addressing their children.'
59	13	5	*Ol papa I save tanim toktok bilong ol taim ol i toktok long pikinini bilong ol.* 'Fathers change their speech when they are addressing their children.'
60	19	0	*Sampela pikinini I kisim tokples hariap, sampela isi isi tasol.* 'Some children learn their vernacular very fast, others just slowly.'
61	20	0	*Taim yu toktok long pikinini bilong yu, yu mas tingim save bilong em: Nogut yu toktok hariap na em i no inap harim.* 'If you talk to your children, you must think about their knowledge. If you talk too fast, they might not understand you.'
62	20	0	*Sapos pikinini bilong yu i paul long tokples, yu mas stretim em.* 'If your child makes language errors, you have to correct them.'
63	19	1	*Sapos pikinini bilong narapela paul long tokples, yu mas stretim em.* 'If other people's children make language errors, you have to correct them.'
64	19	1	*Sapos pikinini bilong yu i miksim tokples wantaim Tok Pisin, yu mas stretim em.* 'If your children mix Qaqet and Tok Pisin, you have to correct them.'

References

Agheyisi, Rebecca & Joshua A. Fishman. 1970. Language attitude studies: A brief survey of methodological approaches. *Anthropological Linguistics* (12). 131–57. www.jstor.org/stable/30029244?seq=1.

Akinyi Ojuondo, Millicent. 2015. *Influence of play on development of language skills among preschool children in Kisumu central sub-county, Kenya*. Nairobi: University of Nairobi. (Doctoral dissertation). hdl.handle.net/11295/92806.

Albert, Aviad, Francesco Cangemi & Martine Grice. 2018. Using periodic energy to enrich acoustic representations of pitch in speech: A demonstration. In *9th International Conference on Speech Prosody 2018*, 804–08. ISCA: ISCA. doi.org/10.21437/SpeechProsody.2018-162.

Albert, Aviad, Francesco Cangemi, Martine Grice & Mark Ellison. 2020. *ProPer: PROsodic analysis with PERiodic energy*. doi.org/10.17605/OSF.IO/28EA5.

Allen, Shanley & Catherine Dench. 2015. Calculating mean length of utterance for eastern Canadian Inuktitut. *First Language* 35(4–5). 377–406. doi.org/10.1177/0142723715596648.

Ambridge, Ben & Elena Lieven. 2013. *Child language acquisition: Contrasting theoretical approaches*. 3rd edn. Cambridge: Cambridge University Press. doi.org/10.1017/CBO9780511975073.002.

Anand, Pranav, Sandra Chung & Matthew Wagers. 2011. Widening the net: Challenges for gathering linguistic data in the digital age. *NFS SBE 2010: Future Research in the Social, Behavioural and Economic Sciences*. 1–5. people.ucsc.edu/~mwagers/papers/WideningtheNet.AnandChungWagers.pdf.

Barnes, Sally, Mary Gutfreund, David Satterly & Gordon Wells. 1983. Characteristics of adult speech which predict children's language development. *Journal of Child Language* 10(01). 65–84. doi.org/10.1017/S0305000900005146.

Bavin, Edith L. 1992. The acquisition of Warlpiri. In Dan I. Slobin (ed.), *The crosslinguistic study of language acquisition*, 309–71. Hillsdale, NJ: Lawrence Erlbaum.

Bavin, Edith L. 2004. Focusing on where. An analysis of Warlpiri frog stories. In Sven Strömqvist & Ludo Th. Verhoeven (eds), *Relating events in narrative*, 17–35. Mahwah, NJ: Lawrence Erlbaum. doi.org/10.4324/9781410609694.

Behrens, Heike (ed.). 2008. *Corpora in language acquisition research: History, methods, perspectives* (Trends in Language Acquisition Research 6). Amsterdam: John Benjamins. doi.org/10.1075/tilar.6.

Bley, Bernhard. 1914. Sagen der Baininger auf Neupommern, Südsee. *Anthropos* (9). 196–220, 418–48.

Boersma, Paul & David Weenink. 2021. *Praat: Doing phonetics by computer* [computer program]. www.praat.org/.

Briggs, Charles L. 1986. *Learning how to ask: A sociolinguistic appraisal of the role of the interview in social science research*. Cambridge: Cambridge University Press. doi.org/10.1017/CBO9781139165990.

Broen, Patricia A. 1972. *The verbal environment of the language learning child* (Monograph of the American Speech and Hearing Association 17). Washington, D.C.: American Speech and Hearing Association.

Broesch, Tanya L. & Gregory A. Bryant. 2014. Prosody in infant-directed speech is similar across western and traditional cultures. *Journal of Cognition and Development* 16(1). 31–43. doi.org/10.1080/15248372.2013.833923.

Brown, Roger. 1973. *A first language: The early stages*. Harvard: Harvard University Press.

Brown, Roger & Camille Hanlon. 1970. Derivational complexity and order of acquisition in child speech. In John R. Hayes & Roger Brown (eds), *Cognition and the development of language*, 11–53. New York: Wiley.

Bruner, Jerome S. 1974. The organization of early skilled action. In Martin P.M. Richards (ed.), *The integration of a child into a social world*, 167–84. London: Cambridge University Press.

Bruner, Jerome S. 1985. *Child's talk: Learning to use language*. New York, London: W.W. Norton & Company.

Bryant, Gregory A. & Clark H. Barrett. 2007. Recognizing intentions in infant-directed speech: Evidence for universals. *Psychological Science* 18(8). 746–51. doi.org/10.1111/j.1467-9280.2007.01970.x.

Bryant, Gregory A., Pierre Liénard & H. Clark Barrett. 2012. Recognizing infant-directed speech across distant cultures: Evidence from Africa. *Journal of Evolutionary Psychology* 10(2). 47–59. doi.org/10.1556/JEP.10.2012.2.1.

Burger, Friedrich. 1913. *Die Küsten- und Bergvölker der Gazellehalbsinsel. Ein Beitrag zur Völkerkunde von Neuguinea unter besonderer Hervorhebung rechtlicher und sozialer Einrichtungen.* Stuttgart: Strecker & Schröder.

Cangemi, Francesco. 2015. *Mausmooth* [computer program]. phonetik.phil-fak.uni-koeln.de/fcangemi.html.

Casillas, Marisa, Penelope Brown & Stephen C. Levinson. 2020a. Early language experience in a Papuan community. *Journal of Child Language* 48(4). 1–23. doi.org/10.1017/S0305000920000549.

Casillas, Marisa, Penelope Brown & Stephen C. Levinson. 2020b. Early language experience in a Tseltal Mayan village. *Child Development* 91(5). 1819–35. doi.org/10.1111/cdev.13349.

Chafe, Wallace L. (ed.). 1980. *The pear stories: Cognitive, cultural, and linguistic aspects of narrative production* (Advances in Discourse Processes 3). Norwood, NJ: Ablex.

Chafe, Wallace L. 1985. Some reasons for hesitating. In Deborah Tannen & Muriel Saville-Troike (eds), *Perspectives on silence*, 77–92. Norwood, NJ: Ablex.

Chafe, Wallace L. 1994. *Discourse, consciousness, and time: The flow and displacement of conscious experience in speaking and writing.* 2nd edn. Chicago: University of Chicago Press.

Chomsky, Noam. 1965. *Aspects of the theory of syntax.* 4th edn. Cambridge, MA: MIT Press.

Chomsky, Noam. 1981. *Lectures on government and binding: The Pisa lectures* (Studies in generative grammar 9). Berlin & New York: Mouton de Gruyter.

Chouinard, Michelle M. & Eve V. Clark. 2003. Adult reformulations of child errors as negative evidence. *Journal of Child Language* 30(3). 637–69. doi.org/10.1017/S0305000903005701.

Clark, Herbert H. & Jean E. Fox Tree. 2002. Using uh and um in spontaneous speaking. *Cognition* 84(1). 73–111. doi.org/10.1016/S0010-0277(02)00017-3.

Clark, Herbert H. & Thomas Wasow. 1998. Repeating words in spontaneous speech. *Cognitive Psychology* 37(3). 201–42. doi.org/10.1006/cogp.1998.0693.

Cristia, Alejandrina, Emmanuel Dupoux, Michael Gurven & Jonathan Stieglitz. 2017. Child-directed speech is infrequent in a forager-farmer population: A time allocation study. *Child Development* 90(3). 759–73. doi.org/10.1111/cdev.12974.

Cross, Toni G. 1977. Mothers' speech adjustments: The contribution of selected child listener variables. In Catherine E. Snow & Charles A. Ferguson (eds), *Talking to children*, 151–88. Cambridge: Cambridge University Press.

Crowley, Terry & Nick Thieberger. 2010. *Field linguistics: A beginner's guide* (Oxford linguistics). Oxford & New York: Oxford University Press.

de León Pasquel, Lourdes. 2011. Language socialization and multiparty participation frameworks. In Alessandro Duranti, Elinor Ochs & Bambi B. Schieffelin (eds), *The handbook of language socialization* (Blackwell Handbooks in Linguistics), 81–111. Malden, MA: WileyBlackwell.

Defina, Rebecca. 2020. Acquisition of Pitjantjatjara clause chains. *Frontiers in Psychology* 11. 541. doi.org/10.3389/fpsyg.2020.00541.

Dickhardt, Michael. 2009. *Schau nur, und also wirst du dich wandeln! Eine Studie zur Kulturanthropologie der Moralität unter den Qaqet-Baining von Raunsepna, Neubritannien, Gazellehalbinsel, PapuaNeuguinea*. Göttingen: Georg-August-Universität Göttingen. (Habilitationsschrift).

Dickhardt, Michael. 2012. Die mit den Geistern tanzen: Maskentänze, Identität und Moral unter den Qaqet-Baining (Gazellehalbinsel, Neubritannien, Papua-Neuguinea). *Mitteilungen der Berliner Gesellschaft für Anthropologie, Ethnologie und Urgeschichte* (33).

Du Bois, John W. 1980. Introduction - The search for a cultural niche: Showing the pear film in a Mayan community. In Wallace L. Chafe (ed.), *The pear stories* (Advances in discourse processes), 1–7. Norwood, NJ: Ablex.

Duranti, Alessandro. 2008. *Linguistic anthropology*. 12th edn. (Cambridge textbooks in linguistics). Cambridge: Cambridge University Press.

Dyers, Charlyn & Jane-Francis Abongdia. 2010. An exploration of the relationship between language attitudes and ideologies in a study of Francophone students of English in Cameroon. *Journal of Multilingual and Multicultural Development* 31(2). 119–34. doi.org/10.1080/01434630903470837.

Eckert, Penelope. 2004. *Linguistic variation as social practice: The linguistic construction of identity in Belten High* (Language in Society 27). Malden, MA: Blackwell Publishing Ltd.

Errington, Joseph. 2008. *Linguistics in a colonial world: A story of language, meaning and power*. Malden, MA: Blackwell Publishing Ltd. doi.org/10.1002/9780470690765.

Fajans, Jane. 1983. Shame, social action, and the person among the Baining. *Ethos* 11(3). 166–80.

Fajans, Jane. 1985. The person in social context: The social character of Baining 'psychology'. In Geoffrey M. White & John Kirkpatrick (eds), *Person, self, and experience*, 367–97. Berkeley: University of California Press.

Fajans, Jane. 1993. *Exchanging products: Producing exchange*. Sydney: Sydney University Press.

Fajans, Jane. 1997. *They make themselves: Work and play among the Baining of Papua New Guinea*. Chicago: University of Chicago Press.

Farrar, Michael J. 1990. Discourse and the acquisition of grammatical morphemes. *Journal of Child Language* 17(03). 607. doi.org/10.1017/S0305000900010904.

Ferguson, Charles A. 1964. Baby talk in six languages. *American Anthropologist* 66(6). 103–14. doi.org/10.1525/aa.1964.66.suppl_3.02a00060.

Fernald, Anne. 1992. Human maternal vocalizations to infants as biologically relevant signals: An evolutionary perspective. In Jerome H. Barkow, John Tooby & Leda Cosmides (eds), *The adapted mind*, 391–449. New York: Oxford University Press.

Fernald, Anne & Claudia Mazzie. 1991. Prosody and focus in speech to infants and adults. *Developmental Psychology* 27(2). 209–21. doi.org/10.1037/0012-1649.27.2.209.

Fernald, Anne & Thomas Simon. 1984. Expanded intonation contours in mothers' speech to newborns. *Developmental Psychology* 20(1). 104–13. doi.org/10.1037//0012-1649.20.1.104.

Fernald, Anne, Traute Taeschner, Judy Dunn, Mechthild Papousek, Bénédicte de Boysson-Bardies & Ikuko Fukui. 1989. A cross-language study of prosodic modifications in mothers' and fathers' speech to preverbal infants. *Journal of Child Language* 16(3). 477–501. doi.org/10.1017/S0305000900010679.

Gallaway, Clare & Brian J. Richards (eds). 1994. *Input and interaction in language acquisition*. Cambridge: Cambridge University Press.

Garnica, Olga K. 1977. Some prosodic and paralinguistic features of speech to young children. In Catherine E. Snow & Charles A. Ferguson (eds), *Talking to children*, 63–88. Cambridge: Cambridge University Press.

Gaskins, Suzanne, Wendy Haight & David F. Lancy. 2007. The cultural construction of play. In Artin Goncu & Suzanne Gaskins (eds), *Play and Development*. Psychology Press.

Gaskins, Suzanne & Ruth Paradise. 2010. Learning through observation in daily life. In David F. Lancy, John C. Bock & Suzanne Gaskins (eds), *The anthropology of learning in childhood*, 85–117. Walnut Creek, CA: AltaMira Press.

Glas, Ludivine, Caroline Rossi, Rim Hamdi-Sultan, Cédric Batailler & Hacene Bellemmouche. 2018. Activity types and child-directed speech: A comparison between French, Tunisian Arabic and English. *Canadian Journal of Linguistics/Revue canadienne de linguistique* 63(4). 633–66. doi.org/10.1017/cnj.2018.20.

Goldman-Eisler, Frieda. 1973. *Psycholinguistics: Experiments in spontaneous speech*. 2nd edn. London: Academic Press.

Golinkoff, Roberta Michnick, Dilara Deniz Can, Melanie Soderstrom & Kathy Hirsh-Pasek. 2015. (Baby)Talk to Me. *Current Directions in Psychological Science* 24(5). 339–44. doi.org/10.1177/0963721415595345.

Gosso, Yumi, Briseida D. Resende & Ana M. A. Carvalho. 2019. Play in South American indigenous children. In Jaipaul L. Roopnarine & Peter K. Smith (eds), *The Cambridge handbook of play*, 322–42. Cambridge: Cambridge University Press. doi.org/10.1017/9781108131384.018.

Gray, Peter. 2019. Evolutionary functions of play. In Jaipaul L. Roopnarine & Peter K. Smith (eds), *The Cambridge handbook of play*, 84–102. Cambridge: Cambridge University Press. doi.org/10.1017/9781108131384.006.

Grenoble, Lenore A. & Lindsay J. Whaley. 2006. *Saving languages: An introduction to language revitalization*. Cambridge (UK) & New York: Cambridge University Press.

Grieser, DiAnne L. & Patricia Kuhl. 1988. Maternal speech to infants in a tonal language: Support for universal prosodic features. *Developmental Psychology* 24. 14–20.

Haggan, Madeline. 2002. Self-reports and self-delusion regarding the use of motherese: Implications from Kuwaiti adults. *Language Sciences* 24(1). 17–28. doi.org/10.1016/S0388-0001(00)00044-9.

Harkness, Sara, Charles Super, Moisés Ríos Bermúdez, Ughetta Moscardino, Jong-Hay Rha, Caroline Johnston Mavridis, Sabrina Bonichini, Blanca Huitrón, Barbara Welles-Nyström, Jesús Palacios, OnKang Hyun, Grace Soriano & Piotr Olaf Zylicz. 2010. Parental ethnotheories of children's learning. In David F. Lancy, John C. Bock & Suzanne Gaskins (eds), *The anthropology of learning in childhood*, 65–81. Walnut Creek, CA: AltaMira Press.

Harkness, Sara M. 1977. Aspects of social environment and language acquisition in rural Africa. In Catherine E. Snow & Charles A. Ferguson (eds), *Talking to children*, 309–15. Cambridge: Cambridge University Press.

Heath, Shirley B. 2009. *Ways with words: Language, life, and work in communities and classrooms*. 18th edn. Cambridge: Cambridge University Press.

Hellwig, Birgit. 2019. *A grammar of Qaqet* (Mouton Grammar Library 79). Berlin: Mouton de Gruyter.

Hellwig, Birgit. 2020. Child language documentation: A pilot project in Papua New Guinea. *Language Documentation & Conservation* 21. 23–52.

Hellwig, Birgit, Carmen Dawuda, Henrike Frye & Steffen Reetz. 2014–19. *Qaqet corpus*.

Hellwig, Birgit & Dagmar Jung. 2020. Child-directed language and how it informs the documentation and description of the adult language. *Language Documentation & Conservation* 14. 188–214.

Henrich, Joseph, Steven J. Heine & Ara Norenzayan. 2010. The weirdest people in the world? *The Behavioral and Bain Sciences* 33(2–3). 61–83, discussion 83–135. doi.org/10.1017/S0140525X0999152X.

Hesse, Karl (ed.). 2007. *A Jos! Die Welt, in der die Chachet-Baininger leben: Sagen, Glaube und Tänze von der Gazelle-Halbinsel Papua-Neuguineas*. Wiesbaden: Harassowitz.

Hesse, Karl & Theo Aerts. 1982. *Baining life and lore*. Port Moresby: University of Papua New Guinea Press.

Hiery, Hermann J. 2007. Die Baininger. Einige historische Anmerkungen zur Einführung. In Karl Hesse (ed.), *A Jos! Die Welt, in der die Chachet-Baininger leben*, vii–xxx. Wiesbaden: Harassowitz.

Himmelmann, Nikolaus P. 2006. The challenges of segmenting spoken language. In Jost Gippert, Nikolaus P. Himmelmann & Ulrike Mosel (eds), *Essentials of language documentation* (Trends in Linguistics. Studies and Monographs), 253–74. Berlin, New York: Mouton de Gruyter.

Himmelmann, Nikolaus P. 2014. Asymmetries in the prosodic phrasing of function words: Another look at the suffixing preference. *Language* 90(4). 927–60. doi.org/10.1353/lan.2014.0105.

Hoenigman, Darja. 2020. Talking about strings: The language of string figure-making in a Sepik society in Papua New Guinea. *Language Documentation & Conservation* Vol. 14 (2020), pp. 598–641.

Hoff-Ginsberg, Erika & Marilyn Shatz. 1982. Linguistic input and the child's acquisition of language. *Psychological Bulletin* 92(1). 3–26. doi.org/10.1037/0033-2909.92.1.3.

Jensen, Lene Arnett & Suzanne Gaskins. 2015. Childhood practices across cultures. In Lene Arnett Jensen (ed.), *The Oxford handbook of human development and culture* (Oxford library of psychology), 185–97. Oxford, New York & Auckland: Oxford University Press. doi.org/10.1093/oxfordhb/9780199948550.013.12.

Jones, Caroline & Felicity Meakins. 2013. The phonological forms and perceived functions of *janyarrp*, the Gurindji 'baby talk' register. *Lingua* 134. 170–93. doi.org/10.1016/j.lingua.2013.07.004.

Keller, Heidi. 2007. *Cultures of infancy*. Mahwah, NJ: Erlbaum.

Keller, Heidi. 2012. Autonomy and relatedness revisited: Cultural manifestations of universal human needs. *Child Development Perspectives* 6(1). 12–18. doi.org/10.1111/j.1750-8606.2011.00208.x.

Kelly, Barbara F., William Forshaw, Rachel Nordlinger & Gillian Wigglesworth. 2015. Linguistic diversity in first language acquisition research: Moving beyond the challenges. *First Language* 35(4–5). 286–304. doi.org/10.1177/0142723715602350.

Kelly, Barbara F. & Rachel Nordlinger. 2014. *Fieldwork and first language acquisition* . In L. Gawne & J. Vaughan (Eds.), Selected papers from the 44th Conference of the Australian Linguistic Society, 2013. Retrieved from bit.ly/ALS2013Proceedings.

Kidd, Celeste, Katherine S. White & Richard N. Aslin. 2011. Toddlers use speech disfluencies to predict speakers' referential intentions. *Developmental Science* 14(4). 925–34. doi.org/10.1111/j.1467-7687.2011.01049.x.

Klimes, Alexa. 2017. *Comparison of various technologies in the acquisition of speech samples for transcription purposes: Listener perception vs. acoustic analysis of signal quality*. University of Northern Iowa. (Doctoral dissertation).

Ko, Eon-Suk. 2012. Nonlinear development of speaking rate in childdirected speech. *Lingua* 122(8). 841–57. doi.org/10.1016/j.lingua.2012.02.005.

Krasnor, Linda Rose & Debra J. Pepler. 1980. The study of children's play: Some suggested future directions. *New Directions for Child and Adolescent Development* 1980(9). 85–95. doi.org/10.1002/cd.23219800908.

Kroskrity, Paul V. 2004. Language ideologies. In Alessandro Duranti (ed.), *A companion to linguistic anthropology* (Blackwell companions to anthropology), 496–517. Malden, MA: Blackwell Publishing Ltd.

Kulick, Don. 1992. *Language shift and cultural reproduction: Socialization, self and syncretism in a Papua New Guinean village.* Cambridge: Cambridge University Press.

Lancy, David F. 2008. *The anthropology of childhood: Cherubs, chattel, changelings.* Cambridge: Cambridge University Press. doi.org/10.1017/CBO9781139680530.

Lancy, David F. 2012a. The chore curriculum. In Gerd Spittler & Michael Bourdillio (eds), *Working and learning among Africa's children*, 23–57. Berlin: Lit Verlag.

Lancy, David F. 2012b. Unmasking children's agency. *AnthropoChildren* 2. 1–19.

Lancy, David F. 2015. Mapping the landscape of children's play. In James E. Johnson, Scott G. Eberle, Thomas S. Henricks & David Kuschner (eds), *The handbook of the study of play*, 431–39. Lanham, Maryland: Rowman & Littlefield.

Lattas, Andrew. 2020. Re-analysing the Baining: The Mytho–Poetics of race, gender and art. *Oceania* 90(2), 98–150. doi.org/10.1002/ocea.5248.

Laufer, Carl P. 1946-1949. Riegenmucha, das Höchste Wesen der Baining. *Anthropos* 41/44(4/6). 497–60.

Laufer, Carl P. 1959. Jugendinitiation und Sakraltänze der Baining. *Anthropos* (54). 905–81.

Levy, Ann K. 1984. The language of play: The role of play in language development. *Early Child Development and Care* 17(1). 49–61. doi.org/10.1080/0300443840170106.

Lieven, Elena. 1994. Crosslinguistic and crosscultural aspects. In Clare Gallaway & Brian J. Richards (eds), *Input and interaction in language acquisition*, 56–73. Cambridge: Cambridge University Press.

Lieven, Elena & Sabine Stoll. 2009. Language. In Marc H. Bornstein (ed.), *Handbook of cultural developmental science*, 143–61. Hove: Psychology.

Lieven, Elena & Sabine Stoll. 2013. Early communicative development in two cultures: A comparison of the communicative environments of children from two cultures. *Human Development* 56(3). 178–206. doi.org/10.1159/000351073.

Lieven, Elena & Michael Tomasello. 2008. Children's first language acquisition from a usage-based perspective. In Peter Robinson & Nick C. Ellis (eds), *Handbook of cognitive linguistics and second language acquisition*, 168–96. New York, NY: Routledge.

MacWhinney, Brian. 2000. *The CHILDES Project: Tools for analyzing talk*. 3rd edn. Mahwah, NJ: Lawrence Erlbaum. doi.org/10.21415/T5G10R.

Marley, Alexandra. 2013. *Language choice amongst the Qaqet Baining: A socialinguistic study of an ethnolinguistic minority in Papua New Guinea*. Melbourne: La Trobe University. (MA thesis).

Mastin, J. Douglas & Paul Vogt. 2015. Infant engagement and early vocabulary development: A naturalistic observation study of Mozambican infants from 1;1 to 2;1. *Journal of Child Language* 43(2). 235–64. doi.org/10.1017/S0305000915000148.

Miller, Jon F. 1981. *Assessing language production in children: Experimental procedures*. Baltimore, MD: University Park Press. doi.org/10.1017/S0142716400004185.

Milroy, Leslie & Matthew Gordon. 2003. *Sociolinguistics. Method and interpretation*. Malden, MA: Wiley Blackwell. doi.org/10.5/12pt.

Nelson, Katherine. 1977. First Steps in Language Acquisition. *Journal of the American Academy of Child Psychiatry* 16(4). 563–83. doi.org/10.1016/S0002-7138(09)61180-8.

Nelson, Katherine. 1996. *Language in cognitive development: The emergence of the mediated mind*. Reprint Cambridge: Cambridge University Press. doi.org/10.1017/CBO9781139174619.

Nelson, Katherine. 2007. *Young minds in social worlds: Experience, meaning, and memory*. Cambridge, MA: Harvard University Press.

Newport, Elissa, Henry Gleitman & Lila R. Gleitman. 1977. Mother, I'd rather do it myself: Some effects and non-effects of maternal speech style. In Catherine E. Snow & Charles A. Ferguson (eds), *Talking to children*, 109–49. Cambridge: Cambridge University Press.

Nilsson Björkenstam, Kristina, Mats Wirén & Robert Eklund. 2013. Disfluency in child-directed speech. In Robert Eklund (ed.), *Proceedings of Fonetik 2013 the XXVIth Swedish Phonetics Conference, Studies in Language and Culture*, 57–60. Linköping.

Ninio, Anat, Catherine E. Snow, Barbara A. Pan & Pamela R. Rollins. 1994. Classifying communicative acts in children's interactions. *Journal of Communication Disorders* 27. 157–78. doi.org/10.1016/0021-9924(94)90039-6.

O'Grady, William Delaney. 2005. *How children learn language* (Cambridge approaches to linguistics). Cambridge: Cambridge University Press.

Ochs, Elinor. 1988. *Culture and language development: Language acquisition and language socialization in a Samoan village*. Cambridge: Cambridge University Press.

Ochs, Elinor & Bambi B. Schieffelin. 1984. Language acquisition and socialization: Three developmental stories and their implications. In Ben G. Blount (ed.), *Language, culture and society*, 276–319. Waveland Press.

Orena, Adriel John & Katherine S. White. 2015. I forget what that's called! Children's online processing of disfluencies depends on speaker knowledge. *Child Development* 86(6). 1701–9. doi.org/10.1111/cdev.12421.

Owens, Sarah J. & Susan A. Graham. 2016. Thee, uhh disfluency effect in preschoolers: A cue to discourse status. *The British Journal of Developmental Psychology* 34(3). 388–401. doi.org/10.1111/bjdp.12137.

Owens, Sarah J., Justine M. Thacker & Susan A. Graham. 2018. Disfluencies signal reference to novel objects for adults but not children. *Journal of Child Language* 45(3). 581–609. doi.org/10.1017/S0305000917000368.

Oxenham, Andrew J. 2012. Pitch perception. *The Journal of Neuroscience: The Official Journal of the Society for Neuroscience* 32(39). 13335–38. doi.org/10.1523/JNEUROSCI.3815-12.2012.

Parker, Diana & Jim Parker. 1974. *Phonologies of four Papua New Guinea languages* (Workpapers in Papua New Guinea Languages 4). Ukarumpa, Papua New Guinea: S.I.L.

Parker, Diana & Jim Parker. 1977. Baining grammar essentials. Ms. 95pp.

Parkinson, Richard. 1907. *Dreissig Jahre in der Südsee*. Stuttgart: Strecker & Schröder.

Peters, Ann M. & Stephen T. Boggs. 1986. Interactional routines as cultural influences upon language acquisition. In Bambi B. Schieffelin & Elinor Ochs (eds), *Language socialization across cultures* (Studies in the Social and Cultural Foundations of Language), 80–96. Cambridge: Cambridge University Press. doi.org/10.1017/CBO9780511620898.004.

Pfeiler, Barbara. 2007. Lo oye, repite y lo piensa: The contribution of prompting to socialization and language acquisition in Yukatek Maya toddlers in Yucatan, Mexico. In Barbara Pfeiler (ed.), *Learning Indigenous Languages: Child Language Acquisition in Mesoamerica* (Studies on Language Acquisition), 183–202. Berlin: Mouton de Gruyter.

Phillips, Juliet R. 1973. Syntax and vocabulary of mothers' speech to young children: Age and sex comparisons. *Child Development* 44(1). 182–85.

Piaget, Jean. 1957. *Construction of reality in the child*. London: Routledge & Kegan Paul.

Pine, Julian N. 1994. The language of primary caregivers. In Clare Gallaway & Brian J. Richards (eds), *Input and interaction in language acquisition*, 15–37. Cambridge: Cambridge University Press.

Pye, Clifton. 1986a. An Ethnography of Mayan speech to children: An ethnography of Mayan baby talk with special reference to Quiché. *Working Papers in Child Language. The Child Language Program, University of Kansas* (1). 30–58.

Pye, Clifton. 1986b. Quiché Mayan speech to children. *Journal of Child Language* 13(01). doi.org/10.1017/S0305000900000313.

Pye, Clifton. 1992. The acquisition of K'iche' (Maya). In Dan I. Slobin (ed.), *The crosslinguistic study of language acquisition*, 221–308. Hillsdale, NJ: Lawrence Erlbaum.

Pye, Clifton. 2020. Documenting the acquisition of indigenous languages. *Journal of Child Language* 48(3). 454–79. doi.org/10.1017/S0305000920000318.

R Core Team. 2018. *R: A language and environment for statistical computing*. R Foundation for Statistical Computing, Vienna, Austria. www.r-project.org/index.html

Rascher, Paul M. 1904. *Grundregeln der Bainingsprache* (Mitteilungen des Seminars für Orientalische Sprachen zu Berlin).

Rascher, Paul M. 1909. *Baining, Land und Leute*. Münster: Verlag der Aschendorff'schen Buchhandlung.

Ratner, Nan Bernstein & Clifton Pye. 1984. Higher pitch in BT is not universal: Acoustic evidence from Quiche Mayan. *Journal of Child Language* 11(3). 515–22. doi.org/10.1017/S0305000900005924.

Remick, Helen. 1976. Maternal speech to children during language acquisition. In Walburga von Raffler-Engel (ed.), *Baby talk and infant speech* (Neurolinguistics). Amsterdam: Swets & Zeitlinger.

Richards, Brian J. & Clare Gallaway. 1994. Conclusions and directions. In Clare Gallaway & Brian J. Richards (eds), *Input and interaction in language acquisition*, 253–69. Cambridge: Cambridge University Press.

Rispoli, Matthew & Pamela Hadley. 2001. The leading-edge. *Journal of Speech Language and Hearing Research* 44(5). 1131. doi.org/10.1044/1092-4388 (2001/089).

Robbins, Joel & Alan Rumsey. 2008. Introduction: Cultural and linguistic anthropology and the opacity of other minds. *Anthropological Quarterly* 81(2). 407–20. doi.org/10.1353/anq.0.0005.

Rogoff, Barbara, Jayanthi Mistry, Artin Göncü, Cristine Mosler, Pablo Chavajay & Shirley B. Heath (eds). 1993. *Guided participation in cultural activity by toddlers and caregivers* (Monographs of the Society for Research in Child Development 5 58(8)).

Rohatynskyj, Marta A. 2000. The enigmatic Baining: The breaking of an ethnographer's heart. In Sjoerd R. Jaarsma & Marta A. Rohatynskyj (eds), *Ethnographic artifacts*, 74–194. Honolulu: University of Hawaii Press.

Rohatynskyj, Marta A. 2001. On knowing the Baining and other minor ethnic groups of East New Britain. *Social Analysis: The International Journal of Social and Cultural Practice* 45(2). 23–40.

Rowe, Meredith L. 2008. Child-directed speech: Relation to socioeconomic status, knowledge of child development and child vocabulary skill. *Journal of Child Language* 35(01).

Rowe, Meredith L. 2012. Recording, transcribing and coding interaction. In Erika Hoff (ed.), *Research methods in child language: A practical guide*, 193–1007. Malden, MA: Wiley-Blackwell.

Rowe, Meredith L. & Catherine E. Snow. 2020. Analyzing input quality along three dimensions: Interactive, linguistic, and conceptual. *Journal of Child Language* 47(1). 5–21. doi.org/10.1017/S0305000919000655.

Sachs, Jacqueline. 1977. Adaptive significance of input to infants. In Catherine E. Snow & Charles A. Ferguson (eds), *Talking to children*, 51–61. Cambridge: Cambridge University Press.

Sarvasy, Hannah. 2019/01/25. *Nungon*. Cologne.

Saxton, Matthew. 1997. The contrast theory of negative input. *Journal of Child Language* (24). 139–61.

Saxton, Matthew. 2009. The inevitability of child directed speech. In Susan H. Foster-Cohen (ed.), *Language acquisition* (Palgrave advances in linguistics), 62–86. Houndmills, Basingstoke, Hampshire England & New York: Palgrave Macmillan.

Saxton, Matthew. 2015. *Child language: Acquisition and development*. Los Angeles, CA: Sage.

Schieffelin, Bambi B. 1990. *The give and take of everyday life: Language socialization of Kaluli children*. 2nd ed. Tucson, AZ: Fenestra Books.

Schieffelin, Bambi B. & Elinor Ochs (eds). 1986. *Language socialization across cultures*. Repr (Studies in the social and cultural foundations of language 3). Cambridge: Cambridge University Press.

Schilling-Estes, Natalie. 2013. *Sociolinguistic fieldwork* (Key Topics in Sociolinguistics). Cambridge: Cambridge University Press. doi.org/10.1017/CBO9780511980541.

Schmidt, Wilhelm. 1905. Die Bainingsprache, eine zweite Papuasprache auf Neupommern. *Globus* 87. 357–58.

Senft, Barbara & Gunter Senft. 2018. *Growing up on the Trobiand Islands in Papua New Guinea: Childhood and educational ideologies in Tauwema* (Culture and Language Use 21). Amsterdam/Philadelphia: John Benjamins Publishing Company. doi.org/10.1075/clu.21.

Shatz, Marilyn & Rochel Gelman. 1973. The development of communication skills: Modifications in the speech of young children as a function of listener. *Monographs of the Society for Research in Child Development* 38(5). 1–38.

Shneidman, Laura A. & Susan Goldin-Meadow. 2012. Language input and acquisition in a Mayan village: How important is directed speech? *Developmental Science* 15(5). 659–73. doi.org/10.1111/j.1467-7687.2012.01168.x.

Smith, Peter K. 2008. *Children and play*. Oxford: Blackwell. doi.org/10.1002/9781444311006.

Snow, Catherine E. 1972. Mothers' speech to children learning language. *Child Development* 43(2). 549–65.

Snow, Catherine E. 1977a. Mothers' speech research: From input to interaction. In Catherine E. Snow & Charles A. Ferguson (eds), *Talking to children*, 31–49. Cambridge: Cambridge University Press.

Snow, Catherine E. 1977b. The development of conversation between mothers and babies. *Journal of Child Language* 4. 1–22. doi.org/10.1017/S0305000900000453.

Snow, Catherine E. 1994. Beginning from baby talk: Twenty years of research on input in interaction. In Clare Gallaway & Brian J. Richards (eds), *Input and interaction in language acquisition*, 3–12. Cambridge: Cambridge University Press.

Snow, Catherine E. 1996. Issues in the study of input. In Paul Fletcher (ed.), *The handbook of child language* (Blackwell Handbooks in Linguistics), 180–93. Oxford: Blackwell Publishing Ltd.

Snow, Catherine E. & Charles A. Ferguson (eds). 1977. *Talking to children: Language input and acquisition: Papers from a conference sponsored by the Committee on Sociolinguistics of the Social Science Research Council (USA)*. Cambridge: Cambridge University Press.

Speelman, Dirk, Adriaan Spruyt, Leen Impe & Dirk Geeraerts. 2013. Language attitudes revisited: Auditory affective priming. *Journal of Pragmatics* 52. 83–92. doi.org/10.1016/j.pragma.2012.12.016.

Spencer, Andrew & Ana R. Luís. 2012. *Clitics: An introduction* (Cambridge Textbooks in Linguistics). Cambridge: Cambridge University Press.

Stanton, Lee. 2007. *Topics in Ura phonology and morphophonology, with lexicographic application.* University of Canterbury. (Doctoral dissertation).

Stebbins, Tonya N. 2004. Mali Baining perspectives on language and culture stress. *International Journal of the Sociology of Language* 2004(169). 161–75. doi.org/10.1515/ijsl.2004.039.

Stebbins, Tonya N. 2009. The Papuan languages of the Eastern Bismarcks: Migration, origins and connections. In Bethwyn Evans (ed.), *Discovering history through language*, 223–43. Canberra: Pacific Linguistics.

Stebbins, Tonya N. 2011. *Mali (Baining) grammar: A language of the East New Britain Province, Papua New Guinea*. Canberra: Pacific Linguistics.

Stehlin, Johannes. 1905/1906. Wörterbuch: Baining – Deutsch: Ms.

Stoll, Sabine. 2015. Crosslinguistic approaches to language acquisition. In Edith Laura Bavin & Letitia R. Naigles (eds), *The Cambridge Handbook of Child Language*, 107–34. Cambridge: Cambridge University Press. doi.org/10.1017/CBO9781316095829.006.

Streeck, Jürgen. 1996. A little Ilokano grammar as it appears in interaction. *Journal of Pragmatics* 26(2). 189–213. doi.org/10.1016/0378-2166(96)00012-4.

Thacker, Justine M., Craig G. Chambers & Susan A. Graham. 2018. Five-year-olds' and adults' use of paralinguistic cues to overcome referential uncertainty. *Frontiers in Psychology* 9. 143. doi.org/10.3389/fpsyg.2018.00143.

Tomasello, Michael. 2003. *Constructing a language: A usage-based theory of language acquisition.* Cambridge: Cambridge University Press.

Tomasello, Michael. 2009. The usage-based theory of language acquisition. In Edith Laura Bavin (ed.), *The Cambridge handbook of child language* (Cambridge handbooks in linguistics), 69–87. Cambridge: Cambridge University Press.

Vaughan, Jill, Gillian Wigglesworth, Deborah Loakes, Samantha Disbray & Karin Moses. 2015. Child-caregiver interaction in two remote Indigenous Australian communities. *Frontiers in Psychology* 6. 514.

Vogt, Paul, J. Douglas Mastin & Diede M.A. Schots. 2015. Communivative intentions of child-directed speech in three different learning environments: Observations from the Netherlands, and rural and urban Mozambique. *First Language* 35(4-5). 341–58.

Volmer, Hermann. 1926. Wörterbuch: Baining-Deutsch: Ms.

Volmer, Hermann. 1928. Grammatik des Bainingschen: Ms.

Vygotsky, L. S. 1978. *Mind in society: The development of higher psychological processes.* Cambridge, MA: Harvard University Press.

Warren-Leubecker, Amy & John Neil Bohannon. 1984. Intonation patterns in child-directed speech: Mother-father differences. *Child Development* 50(4). 1379–85.

Watson-Gegeo, Karen Ann & David W. Gegeo. 1986. Calling-out and repeating routines in Kwara'ae children's language socialization. In Bambi B. Schieffelin & Elinor Ochs (eds), *Language socialization across cultures* (Studies in the social and cultural foundations of language), 17–50. Cambridge: Cambridge University Press. doi.org/10.1017/CBO9780511620898.002.

Weisleder, Adriana & Sandra R. Waxman. 2010. What's in the input? Frequent frames in child-directed speech offer distributional cues to grammatical categories in Spanish and English. *Journal of Child Language* 37(5). 1089–108. doi.org/10.1017/S0305000909990067.

Wickham, Hadley. 2009. *ggplot2: Elegant graphics for data analysis* (Use R). New York, NY: Springer-Verlag New York. doi.org/10.1007/978-0-387-98141-3.

Zwicky, Arnold & Geoffrey K. Pullum. 1983. Cliticization vs. inflection: English N'T. *Language* 59(3). 502–13.

Index

A lower case 'fn' following a page number indicates a footnote.

acquisition
    attitudes towards, 23, 24, 47–53, 61–62, 160
    ceasing of, 61
    consequences of manner of for language endangerment, 23
    functionalist vs. nativist approach, 5–10
    order of languages in, 5
    pace of, 4
    See also language shift
adult language, 3, 9–10, 49, 51, 72, 91, 118, 128, 133, 134, 135, 138, 139, 147, 161
anthropological work on Qaqet people, 12–13, 20, 37
attention
    directing, 123–138
    signalling, 74, 134, 136, 146
attitudes
    toward language, 23–25, 51, 149, 153,
    toward play. *See* play
    See also acquisition, attitudes towards
autonomy, 22, 24, 35, 36, 47, 124, 156
Awiakay (Eastern Sepik Province, PNG), 41

babies. *See* infants
baby talk, 72, 149–150, 152, 158
    stigmatised, 47

backchannelling, 134, 137, 138, 146
Baining languages, 10–11, 149
Baining Mountains, 5, 15
Bohannon, John Neil, 8, 107
Broen, Patricia A., 8. 93–94, 108, 119–120, 123

caregivers, 21, 37, 61–62, 70, 83–84, 100, 155, 160
    children as, 32, 34, 52, 62, 156
cash crops, 5, 15
Casillas, Marisa, 4, 22, 24, 62, 156, 158
Chafe, Wallace L., 66–68, 76–77, 102, 125
CHILDES database, 86, 94
chore curriculum, 26, 30, 62
Chouinard, Michelle M., 139, 147
CLAN software, 87, 125
Clark, Eve V., 139, 147
Clark, Herbert H., 8, 93, 95, 96, 97
cliticisation, 80, 87
code-mixing, 53
Codes for the Human Analysis of Transcripts (CHAT), 75, 86, 87, 88, 95
communal action autonomy, 22, 24, 124, 156
concentration span, 8, 20, 70, 127, 134, 138
consensus, 27
contours

intonation, 77–79, 86, 97, 109, 121, 135, 159
    pitch, 76, 77, 116
correction, 47, 50, 61–62, 139–147, 156
    See also recasts

dispossession, 11
Duranti, Alessandro, 29

East New Britain Province, 11
East Papuan languages, 11
education, formal, 22, 26, 29, 156, 160
    See also play
ELAN software, 55, 75, 95
endangerment. *See* language shift
entire-day-data, 17, 19
errors, 61, 139–140, 143, 146–147
ethnography. *See* anthropological work on Qaqet people

face-to-face interaction, 22
Fajans, Jane, 11–13, 24, 26, 37–38, 40, 50
family structure, 15, 35, 58, 60, 158, 160
fathers, 35, 41, 47–48, 50, 51, 58, 62, 74, 91, 108, 152, 156
Fernald, Anne, 107, 108, 109, 121
Firedance, 52
first language. *See* mother tongue
fluency, 93, 94, 104, 105
food (gathering, preparation), 15, 27, 30–37, 40, 47, 54, 57
Fox Tree, Jean E., 8, 97
French, 107, 139
functionalism, 5, 6, 97

Gallaway, Clare, 7–9, 124, 149, 155
Gapun (PNG), 22fn, 23
gardening. *See* food (gathering, preparation)

Gazelle Peninsula, 6, 11
gendered division in labour, 35
generosity, 30, 46, 47
Goldin-Meadow, Susan, 10, 22fn, 56, 57, 59

Hellwig, Birgit, 3, 4, 5, 11, 12, 16, 19, 26, 34, 40, 49, 66, 74, 76–81, 95, 97, 109, 112, 121, 128, 130, 131, 134, 135
Henrich, Joseph, 4
hesitation, 7, 8–9, 78, 94, 96–97, 99–100, 101–104

Ilokano (Philippines), 97fn
imitation, 34–37, 40, 51, 61, 117, 135, 146–147, 149, 153, 159–160
infants, 23, 24, 35, 39, 41, 47, 48, 150, 153
    infant-directed speech, 48, 50, 61, 107, 108, 150, 156
input, linguistic, 4, 6–7, 9–10, 22, 23–24, 54–60, 62, 155, 157–158
    corrective, 139–147
instruction, explicit, 23, 36, 61, 149, 156
interaction, 5, 7, 18, 21–24, 26, 27, 46–48, 50, 73, 100, 126, 136–138, 158–160
interviewer-bias, 27
intonation
    in child directed speech, 7, 108, 117
    intonation contours, 97, 114–116, 117, 121, 135, 159
    units, 71, 72, 76–79, 85–86, 95, 109–110, 112, 125–127, 128–137
    and utterances, 56, 85–86

Jung, Dagmar, 3, 4, 12, 40

K'iche' Maya (Guatamala), 10, 22fn, 66, 84, 108, 109, 123, 124
Kairak (Baining language), 10
Kaluli (PNG), 9, 22fn, 23, 61, 139
Kamanakam (Qaqet village), 19, 39
Kelly, Barbara F., 16, 68
Ko, Eon-Suk, 84, 86, 87
Kulick, Don, 22fn, 23, 53, 61
Kwara'ae (Solomon Islands), 50

Lancy, David F., 22, 26, 32, 35, 37–38, 61
Language Archive Cologne, 19
language choice, 47, 53
language endangerment. *See* language shift
language shift, 3, 23, 48, 52, 53, 61, 85, 157
Lauje (Indonesia), 97fn
Lieven, Elena, 4, 6, 7fn, 35, 62
listeners, 104, 121, 125, 127, 137, 142, 143, 147
longitudinal corpus, 17, 19, 21, 40, 54, 57, 60, 68, 94, 96

Makolkol (Baining language), 10
Mali (Baining language), 10, 12, 52, 149
Marley, Alexandra, 11, 12, 18, 26, 47, 50, 52, 53, 69, 140, 147
missionaries, 11, 12, 14
mobility, 15, 35
morality, studies on, 12–13, 26, 35, 46
mother tongue, 11, 29
Mozambique (Africa), 10, 22fn

narrators, 68–70, 127, 142, 147
nativism, 5
naturalistic data, 18, 19, 26, 84
Nungon (PNG), 149

participant observation, 17, 18, 21, 30
pauses, 77, 86, 93–98, 101, 108, 119–120
　disfluency, 95–101, 104
　hesitation, 75, 77–78, 101–102, 104
Pear film, 16, 67–68
pitch, 77, 78, 95, 97, 107–109, 112, 1161–117, 121, 159
Pitjantjatjara (Australia), 10, 84, 91, 109, 123
play, 37–47, 61, 156
　'Baining do not play' myth, 13, 26, 37–38
　language games, 37
　as learning, 38–39
　Qaqet attitudes to, 37–39
pointing, 48–49
Pye, Clifton, 3, 4, 10, 82, 84, 107, 108, 123

questionnaires, 17, 18, 39

Ratner, Nan Bernstein, 107, 108
Raunsepna (Qaqet village), 5, 11, 12–15, 18–20
recasts, 8, 139–140, 143–147, 157
respect, 26, 45–47
Richards, Brian J., 7, 8, 9, 124, 149, 155
Rogoff, Barbara, 23, 36
Rossel Island (PNG), 22fn, 23, 24, 62, 156
routines, interactional, 48, 49, 50, 117, 134, 160
rural societies. *See* small-scale societies

Samoa, 9, 22fn, 23, 61
school, 12, 15, 22, 24, 29
sharing, 46, 47
Shneidman, Laura A., 10, 22fn, 56, 57, 59

Shuar hunters (Ecuador), 9–10
siblings, 36, 47, 52, 58, 59, 60, 61–62, 156
   older, 34, 41, 43, 52, 54, 55
   younger, 22, 32, 34
SIL, 12, 76
Simbali (Baining language), 10
small-scale societies, 4, 22, 23, 24, 35, 62, 109, 124, 155, 156, 157
Snow, Catherine E., 4, 6, 7, 8, 73, 83, 84, 86, 87, 93, 94, 123, 137, 160
Solomon Islands, 50
staged data, 16, 17, 19, 20, 60
Stanton, 12, 47, 48, 52, 61
stealing, 47
Stebbins, Tonya N., 10, 11, 12, 52, 149
stimuli, 16, 17, 65, 66–68, 158
Stoll, Sabine, 3, 4, 6, 7
subsistence-based societies. *See* small-scale societies

tag-questions, 131, 133, 134
Tagalog (Philippines), 97fn
Tok Pisin, 5, 11, 23, 26, 29, 47, 48, 52, 52, 53, 69
Tolai (East New Britain), 11
triadic joint attention, 22
Trobriand islanders (PNG), 31, 41
Turkana (northwestern Kenya), 10

Uramot (or Ura; Baining language), 10, 12, 47, 157
urban societies, 4, 22, 23, 35, 37, 59, 108, 124, 133
utterances. *See* intonation and utterances

variation, 4, 5, 9, 12, 55, 71, 126, 139, 155, 160
vernacular loss. *See* language shift

Warlpiri (Australia), 22fn, 50
Warren-Leubecker, Amy, 8, 107, 108
Wasow, Thomas, 93, 95, 96
WEIRD and non-WEIRD societies and languages, 4, 9, 10, 21, 22, 36, 52, 54, 61, 84, 108, 109, 155
Western societies. *See* urban societies
word vs. morpheme, 87
Wumpurrarni English (Australia), 84

Yucatec Maya, 10, 22, 37, 56, 59

www.ingramcontent.com/pod-product-compliance
Lightning Source LLC
Chambersburg PA
CBHW061252230426
43664CB00025B/2933